SKATING ON THE SEA

Other translations from Finnish by Keith Bosley

Finnish Folk Poetry: Epic (1977)
Eino Leino: *Whitsongs* (1978)
The Kalevala (1989)
The Kantelatar: a selection (1992)
The Great Bear: Finno-Ugrian oral poetry (1993)
Aleksis Kivi: *Odes* (1994)

SKATING
ON THE SEA
Poetry from Finland

EDITED & TRANSLATED BY
Keith Bosley

BLOODAXE BOOKS
FINNISH LITERATURE SOCIETY

ISBN: 1 85224 388 0 Bloodaxe Books
       951 746 004 X Finnish Literature Society

First published 1997
in the UK by
Bloodaxe Books Ltd,
P.O. Box 1SN,
Newcastle upon Tyne
NE99 1SN.

in Finland by
Finnish Literature Society,
Hallituskatu 1,
00170 Helsinki,
Finland.

Bloodaxe Books Ltd acknowledges
the financial assistance of Northern Arts.

Cover printing by J. Thomson Colour Printers Ltd, Glasgow.

Printed in Great Britain by
Cromwell Press Ltd, Broughton Gifford, Melksham, Wiltshire.

The ice in the vodka
swivels
                and we are heading
north-east, not on pilgrimage
to any womb that shaped
the pillars, the arches of our world
but on safari, though this
is Europe still, to an extremity
a hand extended to the cold.

Below across the Baltic
winter is trailing its cloak before the sun
and we descend out of the blue
upturned bowl on which the old tale tells
there is no hammer mark
towards a land of granite
harrowed by ancient frost
into lake and forest.

Here man came from the east
to drop a net into sweet water
to make a pact with the bear
to build beside his field a house of wood
a bench from wall to wall under the windows
a great stove where the old could chat
and on the shore a sauna
where the new could meet the world

to spin a yarn, to store it
in the shed loft and after bread and beer
to unwind it from here to here
commanding with his tongue
the elk of grass and flowers, the horse of flame
the swan of shadows
                and beyond
the smith who forged the sky
and this child, this milk-beard.

ACKNOWLEDGEMENTS

Acknowledgements are due to the following poets: Gösta Ågren, Claes Andersson, Helena Anhava, Tuomas Anhava, Bo Carpelan, Jorma Etto, Paavo Haavikko, Eila Kivikkaho, Aila Meriluoto, Lassi Nummi, Aale Tynni; to the following publishers: in Finland, Art House, Otava, Schildts, Suomalaisen Kirjallisuuden Seura (Finnish Literature Society), Söderströms, Tammi, Werner Söderström Osakeyhtiö, and in the UK, The Menard Press and Oxford University Press (the latter for translations of the *Kalevala* and the *Kanteletar*, published in the World's Classics); and to the estates of the following: Gunnar Björling, Elmer Diktonius, Rabbe Enckell, Bertel Gripenberg, Aaro Hellaakoski, Helvi Juvonen, Arvi Kivimaa, V.A. Koskenniemi, Larin-Kyösti, Joel Lehtonen, Toivo Lyy, Eeva-Liisa Manner, Otto Manninen, Arvid Mörne, P. Mustapää, L. Onerva, Pentti Saarikoski, Solveig von Schoultz, Katri Vala. Acknowledgements are also due to the periodicals *Books from Finland* (Helsinki) and *World Literature Today* (Norman, Oklahoma). Some translations were commissioned by the late Jeremy Parsons to accompany music recordings; the translation from Juhana Cajanus was commissioned by the Uuno Klami Society.

Publication of this book was made possible through a grant from the Finnish Ministry of Education, thanks to the personal interest of Kalervo Siikala.

The cover reproduces *Winter Landscape* (1880) by Fanny Churberg, in the Ateneum, Helsinki (photo Finnish National Gallery/ Central Art Archives, photographer Hannu Aaltonen).

The poem overleaf was commissioned by *Kaleidoscope* (BBC Radio 4), broadcast and printed in *The Listener*.

CONTENTS

TO THE READER

She makes music, the fine lass
the lass on the lakeshore lilts
with her fine music
with her sombre throat
with her bright spirit.

That fragment was sung in 1837 in south-east Finland, somewhere near Imatra. The singer was an illiterate peasant who may or may not have composed it, for oral tradition is concerned with performance, not authorship. The lyric is a tiny speck in the vast edifice raised by Finnish scholars as *The Old Songs of the Finnish People*: from its thirty-three fat volumes, this is no.1776 of volume 13. The scholar who wrote it down was Elias Lönnrot, compiler from oral sources of the *Kalevala* epic and its lyric companion the *Kanteletar*.

The Finns are a small nation with a small literature now growing by leaps and bounds. Their language is outside the Indo-European family, which stretches from Gaelic to Bengali; it is closely related to Estonian, and distantly to Hungarian. Their poetry is simultaneously among the oldest and youngest: the oral tradition goes back some two thousand years to the Iron Age in Europe (though there are elements from the Stone age), whereas the earliest literary texts date from the mid-16th century.

The oral tradition is astonishing: alliterative, unrhymed, nonstrophic and nearly always in the same metre (a kind of trochaic tetrameter), it ranges from lyrics through charms, proverbs, laments, songs to accompany feasts and rites of passage, narrative songs like our ballads telling of terrible events on the home front, to epic songs about mythical heroes negotiating through magic with spirits believed to control the natural world; the longest epic song recorded from a single performance – just over 400 lines – is in this book (p.47). The tradition was already dying when scholars, seeing in it a validation of their concept of nationhood, began writing it down and studying it about 200 years ago; but by the end of the 19th century it had yielded to its greatest enemy – education. Any oral tradition depends on illiteracy, which is why oral traditions further west have played second fiddle to literary traditions since the late Middle Ages. In Finland for centuries it was the other way round, with the greatest talents remaining unschooled.

As might be expected, Finnish oral tradition gave Christianity a mixed reception. Around 1155 the Swedish king Erik Jedvardsson ('the Good') and the bishop of Uppsala, one Henry (apparently an Englishman, who became Finland's patron saint) launched a mission

that brought Christianity – and Swedish rule – to Finland; a poem
in oral style (p.23) commemorates Henry's martyrdom in fittingly
gruesome terms. The Roman and later the Lutheran Church (the
transition was achieved without bloodshed) did their best to stamp
out the pagan tradition, which continued to flourish in the east of
the country. Here, under the more indulgent eye of Russian Ortho-
doxy, epic songs about pagan heroes coexisted with epic songs
about Jesus:

> When the Creator was killed
> and the Almighty destroyed
> the rocks were heaped under him
> rocks under, the slabs on top
> the gravel against the heart.
>
> [p.58]

The biggest single contributor to the tradition was a woman of
Ingria (south of the Gulf of Finland) whose Lutheran pastor wrote
down 1343 songs from her singing; Larin Paraske (1833/4-1904;
see p.136) had a profound effect on the young Sibelius, who met
her while he was working on *Kullervo*.

The Finnish language was first written in the mid-16th century,
when Bishop Mikael Agricola of Turku (the old capital on the
south-west coast) published an ABC book and translations of the
New Testament and other religious texts (see p.21). Other divines
adapted the metre of the pagan tradition to their own ends. The
most powerful was Juhana Cajanus (1655-81), who gave Finland
its great Baroque poem, a chilling meditation on death:

> He casts, wastes, he crumbles, smashes,
>   Wrings to ashes
> In his stern, his dreadful grasp:
> Hope has fled from the beliefs
>   And the griefs
> Of the mouths that scream and gasp.
>
> [p.27]

Cajanus was accused of a despair learnt from Descartes, who had
settled and died in Sweden; and yet the poem regularly appears in
Finnish hymn books.

While written Finnish was developed mainly for the improve-
ment of the peasantry – the first Finnish grammar (1649) bravely
attempted to describe the language in Latin terms – the language of
power and higher education was Swedish, and a Swedish-language
university was founded in Turku in 1640. Even today, Finns often
refer ironically to the descendants of their former rulers as *bättre*

(better) *folk*. One of the first Finns to write in Swedish was Frans Michael Franzén (1772-1847), who sets forth 'The Ages of Life' in an Alcaic ode that concludes:

> In friendship share your bread with the weary one,
> put out the lamp in silence and sleep in peace
>   until a morning with no evening
>   wakes you anew to eternal springtime.
>
> [p.64]

Franzén was one of a group of writers and scholars known as the Turku Romantics. Among many small nations of eastern Europe, Romanticism was largely political: its ideas of freedom and self-determination were taken up by a growing educated class anxious to shake off foreign rule – Russian, Austro-Hungarian, Ottoman. Finland had been a province of Sweden till 1809, when it was annexed by Russia as an autonomous Grand Duchy. Over the next twenty years the tsar moved both the capital and the university nearer home – and further from Sweden – to Helsinki. He also encouraged the growing nationalist movement as another way of severing links with Sweden. The leader of the Turku Romantics, the journalist Adolf Ivar Arwidsson, famously declared in his newspaper: 'Swedes we are not, Russians we cannot become, so let us be Finns.'

Meanwhile poetry was being written – as well as composed orally – in Finnish. Outside the sphere of improving divines, an anonymous poem in oral metre (1777; p.38) wittily protests at a royal ban on the home manufacture of spirit alcohol, and Pietari Makkonen (1785-1851), one of several peasant poets, has left us a remarkable allegory (p.71) about the emergence of Finnish as a literary medium. The language is presented as a country girl with few rights in law till the 'lords in Helsinki' adopt her. Here the poet draws on wedding songs from oral tradition: the bride's garments, brought at great cost from far away places, become dialect words incorporated into a central language. We leave her 'in a drawing-room...properly herself...with some fine books in her hand'. Now, the poet tells us, she can stand up to any Swedish 'damsel' (*ryökkinä*, from Swedish *fröken*, cf. German *Fräulein*). The 'lords in Helsinki' were the founders of the Finnish Literature Society, formed in 1831 to publish the *Kalevala* and still going strong.

The publication of Elias Lönnrot's *Kalevala* (1835, final version 1849; my translation, 1989) and his *Kanteletar* (1840-1; my translated selection, 1992) at first dismayed educated Finns, because they were in the language these had left behind; but it was the language

of the future. Nevertheless, the language of the past was far from
neglected. Lönnrot's friend Johan Ludvig Runeberg (1804-77) is
still regarded as the 'national poet' because of his *Tales of Ensign
Stål*, a collection of ballads about the war of 1808-9 which ended
Swedish rule; its prologue became the national anthem. He was
much set to music by Sibelius, whose mother tongue was Swedish,
and much admired (in translation) by Brahms, who on hearing the
young Finn's setting of 'Since then I have asked no more' (p.119)
grunted *Aus dem wird was* ('He'll get on'). Zachris Topelius (1818-
98), the father of children's literature in Finland, wrote a 'Christ-
mas Song' (p.128) which every Finn knows in Sibelius' setting,
and in later life two landscape poems (p.129) whose hard-edged
visual realism anticipates the Imagists by some thirty years. Around
the turn of the century, Swedish-speaking Finnish poets, aware that
they were in an ever-dwindling minority, identified themselves
increasingly with the marine landscape of south-western and western
Finland opposite Sweden, leaving the interior with its lakes and
forests – and its oral tradition – to Finnish speakers.

These, after the *Kalevala* and *Kanteletar*, were making up for lost
time, building a written tradition that would temper the sometimes
bookish language of the divines with the racier rural speech of the
people. Here two figures are fatefully linked. August Ahlqvist
(1826-89) not only venerated the *Kalevala* – he made a concordance
of it – and travelled round north-east European Russia studying
oral traditions in languages related to Finnish; he also visited central
and southern Europe, bringing back ideas and forms from little
understood Renaissance cultures. As a poet writing under the name
of A. Oksanen, he introduced the German-style Romantic ballad:
'The Rapid-Shooter's Brides' (p.133) was set to music by Sibelius.
He also wrote the first sonnet in Finnish (1854; p.135) in which he
urges his countrymen to follow his example and so inspire inter-
national respect for their language.

His younger contemporary Aleksis Kivi (1834-72) saw things
differently. Also recognising the need to work in new forms, he
went to the grass roots and devised a new prosody based on speech
(a little like Hopkins) in which rhyme, that badge of cultural
respectability, had virtually no place. He wrote the first Finnish
plays (his *Kullervo* is the basis of the opera by Aulis Sallinen) and
the first Finnish novel, *Seven Brothers* (1870). It was Ahlqvist's
rubbishing of this pioneering work that hastened Kivi's early death.
His prosodic experiments, like Hopkins', had few followers, but
his poems – bland though many of them may be to some tastes –

are constantly reprinted, and his novel is regarded as a classic. (For
a discussion of Kivi the poet, see my translated selection, *Odes*,
Helsinki, 1994.)

When Kivi died, Paavo Cajander (1846-1913) wrote a Sapphic
ode in his memory – a delicate gesture combining Kivi's unrhymed
homespun with a wider world beyond Oksanen's sonnet. Finnish
poets were already imitating classical metres on the German
model, converting quantity to stress; there are some examples in
this book, most curiously from Lönnrot, who echoes the home-
sickness of Ovid's *Tristia* as he collects material for the *Kalevala*
in deepest Karelia (p.86). Cajander is mainly remembered for his
translations of Runeberg and most of Shakespeare.

Another great translator is one of two poets who emerged at the
turn of the century and are now acquiring an international reputa-
tion. Otto Manninen (1872-1950) translated Homer, Goethe,
Runeberg, Petőfi and much else; his own poems show him to be a
kind of Finnish Valéry, and perhaps the most challenging Finnish
poet to translate. Whereas the timeless moment celebrated in *Le
Cimetière marin* has a human setting, with nature supplying only a
backdrop, that of 'Still Waters' is entirely in the natural world:

> Glisten with summer's blessing, lest
> a notion gnaw us to be hence,
> to pass down through the whirlpool's rage,
> through the most final confluence.
>
> [p.167]

Eino Leino (1878-1926) is generally regarded as the greatest poet
of Finnish written tradition. The deference to oral tradition per-
sists, as he was the first to maintain: his masterpiece, *Whitsongs*
(1903), is a book of narrative poems in oral style. His St George,
going to rescue the girl from the dragon, finds her in its bed:

> He killed the smiling woman
> with his sword of fiery edge,
>   Saint George the high-born,
> the flower of all Christendom.
>
> [p.181]

Leino's protean but tormented genius was apparent already in his
late teens; his famous poem 'The Swing of the Gods' (p.174),
written in his early twenties, suggests a manic-depressive person-
ality that was to slip into decline by his thirtieth year.

During the early years of Manninen and Leino, less enlightened
Russian authorities decided that the Grand Duchy was getting
above itself; but their oppressive measures (which prompted, for

example, Sibelius' *Finlandia*) only increased the urge to independence, finally achieved in 1917 when Russia had upheavals of its own. At the time, a third major – but very short-lived – talent was developing. Of Finnish nationality, of Finland-Swedish descent, born in Russia but brought up speaking German, Edith Södergran (1892-1923) committed to Swedish a vision of life that made her a forerunner of Finnish Modernism and of modern feminist attitudes. Finnish women were, after all, the first in Europe to have equal rights with men – in 1906, eleven years before independence:

> You sought a flower
> and found a fruit.
> You sought a spring
> and found a sea.
> You sought a woman
> and found a soul –
> you are disappointed.
>
> [p.198]

Södergran's elder by five years, Gunnar Björling (1887-1960), has been described as 'Scandinavia's only Dadaist': with Elmer Diktonius (1896-1961) and Rabbe Enckell (1903-74), these four, plus Runeberg, are the only Finland-Swedish poets accepted in the Swedish canon. A few later poets, like Solveig von Schoultz (1907-96) and Bo Carpelan (born 1926), are known beyond their native shores. No wonder that today's Finland-Swedish writers find kindred spirits among southern African writers of English.

Another forerunner of Finnish Modernism was Aaro Hellaakoski (1893-1952), though his early poem 'Conceptio Artis' (p.201) looks back to the 1890s, when the 'national' painter Gallen-Kallela and his circle – which included Sibelius – held drunken all-night sessions on what art was all about; they were much in the spirit of Symbolism, which Russia took up when the French were tired of it. Hellaakoski's poem bears the title of a painting Gallen-Kallela destroyed: it showed a naked man attempting to rape a sphinx, to subject art to his will; we are a long way here from seducing the muse. After the Finnish Republic's bloody baptism in the civil war of 1918, Hellaakoski turned to France for models: his poems of the 1920s (p.202) show the influence of Apollinaire and Reverdy, paving the way to developments thirty years later.

As any student of literature knows, translation plays a crucial role when a nation is putting itself on the cultural map. In Finland this happened from the mid-19th century onwards: to Cajander and Manninen already mentioned must now be added – among others – Toivo Lyy (1898-1976), who translated the *Nibelungenlied* and a fair chunk of the *Canterbury Tales*, and Aale Tynni (born 1913), whose anthology *A Thousand Years of Songs* presents Western lyric poetry from Old Norse via the Americas and the Mediterranean (but excluding the Slavs) to modern Swedish; both poets are represented here (pp.206, 215).

Tynni's husband Martti Haavio (1899-1973) was a distinguished folklorist, who as P. Mustapää was also a poet associated with the Torchbearers, a leftwing group in the 1930s. Probably of most lasting value among these is Katri Vala (1901-44), whose freer forms look forward to what was to come; her work continued a feminine presence in a literature still noteworthy for its women practitioners. Later women poets include Helvi Juvonen (1919-59), whose work inhabits a beast-haunted world reminiscent of the Austrian poet Ingeborg Bachmann, Eeva-Liisa Manner (1921-95), a poet of loss and loneliness, and Helena Anhava (born 1925), who with her husband Tuomas (born 1927) spearheaded the Modernist movement and introduced Oriental poetry – a late parallel with Ezra Pound – translated by Tuomas.

Swedish-speaking poets absorbed more European influences – Expressionism, Dada, Surrealism: their language is better fitted for abrupt changes of theme and mood. But Bo Carpelan has described the writing of poetry as 'listening with the eyes' – an indication of his debt to Imagism; and his younger contemporary Gösta Ågren (born 1936) brings us an even sharper glimpse of life in deprived areas of Ostrobothnia to the north-west, a glimpse heightened – he claims – by reading R.S. Thomas, who has written of a similar community divided by language.

Since the Nobel Prize for Literature was awarded in 1939 to the novelist F.E. Sillanpää, the biggest international award to a Finnish writer has been the Neustadt Prize (the 'American Nobel'), presented in 1984 to the poet, playwright and novelist Paavo Haavikko (born 1931). The leading light of Finnish Modernism, Haavikko remains an intensely private figure, declaring – in the best Symbolist manner – that the work is the man. Obsessed with history and power politics, with the occasional interlude of personal pain, much of his huge output is a mystery to a public accustomed to its writers speaking either on its behalf or on their own:

> Let the sweet memory of you also fade, die, go away,
>   for now that you have fully settled into a dream
> and dwell there,
>   meeting there is pointless, painful, a parting.

[p.230]

Pentti Saarikoski (1937-83) was the *enfant terrible* of Modernism, but behind this mask is an awesome achievement in translation that includes the *Odyssey* and Joyce's *Ulysses*. Saarikoski's poems, scattered across the page, seem to enact the confused idealism of his generation. With him, as with a handful of other poets represented in this book, one has the feeling of a great talent trapped in a small language – which is the best justification for the labours of a translator; but we also need to go beyond such star performers to get an idea of what makes a nation tick, especially one with a reputation for being – as Brecht said – silent in two languages.

Current thinking in Finland regards Finnish literature as a bilingual unit; but it has always been and remains two literatures with their own cultures and traditions, rather like English and Celtic. Here, for better or worse, they are together: while the English mind might boggle at an anthology that presented Chaucer and Dafydd ap Gwilym as bedfellows, this book reflects a young nation whose attitude to its linguistic minority is an example to the world.

The anthology was going to be bigger than it is, but I reduced it by a third because I feared that my zeal for being representative might err towards the parochial. So I have concentrated on good poems (of course), famous poems (though I may not always like them), and poems I personally like (though others may not). An anthologist must stop somewhere: I chose to stop at the latest poet to attract wide international attention. With so much poetry of the past here making its first appearance in English, I have tried to bring it to life by imitating – rather than reproducing or disregarding – its forms, but at the same time speaking for it in the language of today. This approach was first described in Britain in the 16th century by Gavin Douglas, whose 'rurall vulgar gros' gave speakers of English for the first time 'sum savoryng' of the *Aeneid*.

Finally, my thanks go first to Marja-Leena Rautalin of the Finnish Literature Information Centre, to Matti Suurpää and Senni Timonen of the Finnish Literature Society, to my former BBC colleague Essi Kiviranta and to my wife Satu Salo. Any lapses in taste or accuracy remain my responsibility.

KEITH BOSLEY
Upton-cum-Chalvey

MIKAEL AGRICOLA

from Preface to the Psalter

Many heathen gods there were
  worshipped of old, both far and near.
To these the folk of Häme bowed then –
  not only women but also men:
Tapio from forests granted game
  and Achti from waters did the same;
Äinemöinen fashioned verses
  and Rachkoi fixed the moon's courses;
Lieckiö ruled grasses, roots and trees
  and many other things like these;
Ilmarinen over skies held sway
  and guided travellers on their way;
Turisas vouchsafed victory,
  Kratti took care of property;
Tontu kept order in the house
  while the devil was running loose;
And maiden spirits devoured the moon
  and giants struck the harvest down.

Now here are the heathen gods displayed
  to whom the folk of Karelia prayed:
Rongoteus gave them rye,
  Fieldpeter raised the barley high;
Wirankannos looked after oats
  and much else that went down their throats;
Egres grew peas, beans, turnips too,
  cabbages, flax, hemp he saw through;
Köntös created clearing and field,
  as their heathen confession held;
And at the end of the spring sowing
  then the Old Man's brew was flowing
And the Old Man's barrel sank
  as both maid and matron drank
And many shameful acts occurred
  as the eye saw and the ear heard;
When Rauni the Old Man's wife would scold
  the Old Man foamed and brought the cold
Out of the north, with the new year
  and the coupling of beasts in the byre;

Hijsi granted the hunter's wish,
　　the Water-mother filled nets with fish;
Nyrckes gave squirrels from the firs,
　　Hittauanin from bushes brought hares.
Are not a people's wits astray
　　who trust in these and to them pray?
By the devil and sin they were pressed
　　so to bow the knee and put their trust.
On the graves of the dead a feast they kept
　　and there lamented, shrieked and wept;
To earth spirits offerings too were made
　　when widows a second time were wed;
To much else also they bowed down –
　　to rocks, treestumps, stars and the moon.

Likewise of late beneath Rome's heel
　　in public and private they would kneel
Before creatures numberless
　　as equals of God in holiness:
To fire, water, earth they bowed their head,
　　to branches, trees, bones of the dead;
Salt, eggs, grass and flesh were adored
　　in sanctuaries of the LORD.
Can any man count all the follies
　　to which the people clung for solace?

Now as to worship, let none share it
　　with Father, Son and Holy Spirit:
That Trinity in Jesus Christ
　　is whole and total, as we trust;
As all the Bible testifies
　　so David here in the Psalter says.
If you should take this book and read
　　and love it and keep it in your head
With its fruits now and all your life through,
　　Christ will grant his grace to you.
So in your prayers remember those
　　who dressed these psalms in Finnish clothes:
The work was done in Turku town,
　　in Saint Laurence House it was writ down;
There my son Christian first saw the light
　　while the LORD worked through us his might,
To whom endless thanks let us give,
　　Amen say every man alive.

TRADITIONAL

A Ballad About St Henry, First Bishop of Turku, who had been born in England

Long ago two children grew
one grew up in Cabbageland
the other rose in Sweden:
one was Henry of Häme
the other Eric the king.
   Henry of Häme
said to Eric his brother:
'Let us go and christen lands
to the unchristened countries
to the places without priests.'

   Then Eric the king
said to Henry his brother:
'What if the lakes have no ice
the winding river's melted?'

And Henry of Häme said:
'So we circle Kiulo Lake
go round the winding river.
Put the colts into harness
fit the yearlings with bridles
and put the sleighs in order
   and line up the struts
to their runners fit wide shafts
the small bright-worked parts behind.'

   At once they drove off.
So they drove one day in spring
   two nights in a row
   and Eric the king
said to Henry his brother:
'Now we are getting hungry
neither eating nor drinking
   no stop for a meal.'
'Lalli is beyond the bay
the fortunate on the cape:
there we shall eat, there we'll drink
   there stop for a meal.'

Then, when they got there
Kerttu the idle mistress
   steamed with her vile mouth
   used her worthless tongue:
at that Henry of Häme
   took hay for the horse
   left coins in its place
   took bread off the stove
   left coins in its place
took beer out of the cellar
and rolled money in its place.
There they ate and there they drank
   there stopped for a meal.
   And soon they drove off.

   Lalli came homeward.
That Lalli's evil mistress
   steamed with her vile mouth
   used her worthless tongue:
   'Men have passed this way:
here they ate and here they drank
   here stopped for a meal
   took hay for the horse
and left sand-grains in its place
   took bread off the stove
and left sand-grains in its place
took beer out of the cellar
and rolled gravel in its place.'

A herdsman spoke from the post
'Now you are just telling lies! –
   Don't you believe her!'

   Lalli, ill-behaved
from an evil family too
Lalli took up his hatchet
the devil took his long spear
and drove off after the lord.

   Then the faithful man
said, the servant to his lord:
'There is a thudding back there:
shall I drive this horse faster?'

Henry of Häme answered:
'If there's a thudding back there
do not drive this horse faster
do not push the steed harder:
hide in the shade of a rock
listen from behind the rocks.
    And when I am caught
    or else even killed
pick my bones out of the snow
and put them on an ox-sledge:
it will draw me to Finland.
    Where the ox grows tired
there let a church be put up
    a chapel be built
for priests to preach sermons in
that all the people may hear.'

Then Lalli returned homeward.
A herdsman spoke from the post:
'Where did Lalli get the cap
the bad man the good helmet
the gallows-bird the mitre?'

Then Lalli the murderer
snatched the cap from off his head:
    his hair came with it.
Pulled the ring off his finger:
his finger-sinews slid off.

So to this ill-behaved one
to the dear bishop's maimer
came the vengeance from on high
payment from the world's ruler.

MATIAS SALAMNIUS

from A Glad Song About Jesus

CHAPTER 24: *On Jesus' Descent into Hell*

When the third morning arrived
the Lord takes his spirit back
   from the Father's hand
and walked in the lanes of death
in the Demon's fields wandered.
The evil place is surprised
by the Creator of all
walking: it slammed its gates hard
   the doors it locked fast
that he might not get inside –
the Most Evil feared his power.
   Jesus steps nearer
close to the devils' stronghold
   kicked the wide gate in
   slammed the doorposts down:
the lock flew into the snow
and the nails burst into flame
the bolts into the same fire.
   He seized some shackles
to put evil ones in them:
he put scoundrels in shackles
and wicked hell he scattered
so that it could nevermore
of itself do anything
to the friends of the Lord, to
the children of the great God.
The most evil place trembled
the Demon's pillars sweated
when the fair Creator walked
showed his steadfast victory
as well as his mighty strength.

JUHANA CAJANUS

An Hymn, Wherein the Transience of this World Is Set Forth, and Also How Man May Console Himself Against Death

Wretched man, are you not made
      Sore afraid
Since you weep throughout the night,
Since you sorrow patiently,
      Helplessly
When black Death reveals his might?

He well knows, the killer foe,
      Where to go
When God's creatures must be found –
Good and evil with their strong ones,
      With their young ones –
To be stuffed into the ground.

He casts, wastes, he crumbles, smashes,
      Wrings to ashes
In his stern, his dreadful grasp:
Hope has fled from the beliefs
      And the griefs
Of the mouths that scream and gasp.

Let us put away their cries,
      Let our eyes
Turn to where the world's ways tend.
Look at all things worth our stares
      And our ears:
Is there nothing that will end?

Do we know of none that die,
      Pass away,
Other than humanity?
In the wind, the stars beyond,
      Sea and land,
Mortals have their company.

What upon the earth goes creeping
      Or goes stepping
Must to earth change after all;
What upon a tree top whistles
      Or but rustles
From the tree at last must fall.

Fly, bird, but how far soever
      You will never
Pass Death's hands; for he will bring,
Merciless, his flying quarry
      In a hurry,
He will catch it on the wing.

Where's a body sturdier,
      Hardier
Than a fish's in a lake?
And yet Doom will slay, will slaughter
      In the water
Water's brood – make no mistake!

Little fishes quickly come
      To their tomb
In the grim pike's gaping jaw,
While the pike's tomb is the hot
      Cooking-pot
And, again, the speaker's maw.

Slender grasses lose their power
      Though they are
Handsome in their blossom-time;
Trees have, whether slight or stout,
      No way out
But are cut down in their prime.

Solid rocks in mountain chains
      Or on plains
Crumble finally to soil,
Iron that destruction brings
      To all things
Rust at last will wreck and spoil.

There is no small thing so faint,
          Impotent,
As great Doom may let it slip,
There is no strong thing so forceful,
          So resourceful,
As may long endure his grip.

If to heaven you cast your gaze
          For his ways,
God will show you in reply
Turning and returning, whirling,
          Twisting, twirling
Stars in the resplendent sky.

One day they will turn from turning
          And returning,
Turn until their turnings cease,
Turn at the imperious word
          Of the Lord
Into void and waywardness.

Thus the heavens will expire
          All on fire
In the stronghold of the stars,
Thus at death the beautiful
          Sun will cool
And the warrior with his wars.

So there's nothing that will last
          Or stand fast
On this world's fast-moving road:
All things fall and all things alter,
          All things falter
Where all things were made by God.

Animate, inanimate
          Do not fret
But to nature's law they bend,
For as hour and day and year
          Disappear
They draw closer to their end.

Let this be your recollection,
       Your reflection,
Sinful man, by day and night,
And from this too take your bearing,
       Not despairing
When Doom comes and fills with fright.

To its death goes every creature
       With its nature
Irrespective: is it then
Such a wonder that you must
       Come to dust
With your sins, you sack of sin?

What's the joy to have a carriage
       And a marriage
In a city doomed to die?
What joy to be permanent
       Resident
In this state of vanity?

Seek another way of living
       And surviving,
And on heaven set your sights!
Seek a way that will not alter
       Neither falter,
And aspire to heaven's delights!

There is joy more plentiful,
       Prodigal,
There delight that will not die,
You will sing there with your young ones,
       With your strong ones
Tireless songs of victory.

But because mankind must die,
       Pass away,
Or he cannot there alight,
Your poor sinful heart is made
       Sore afraid,
Sorrowing at Doom's great might.

FROM ORAL TRADITION

The Singer

She makes music, the fine lass
the lass on the lakeshore lilts
   with her fine music
   with her sombre throat
   with her bright spirit.

Missing Him

If the one I know came now
the one I've seen were in sight
I'd go a mile to meet him
   by boat on water
   on skis through backwoods
   to lift up a fence
   to unlatch a gate:
I would tear brushwood fences
iron fences I'd bring down.
   I would touch his hand
though a snake were in his palm
   I'd climb on his neck
though death were upon his neck
   I would kiss his mouth
though his mouth bled from a wolf
and to his side I would go
though his side were all bloody.

To the Bridegroom

Pure is the bunting on snow
purer is the one you have
bright is the star in the sky
brighter is the one you wed
white on the sea is the froth
whiter is the one you hold
fair on the sea is the duck
fairer is the one you keep.

A Secret Bond

Alas for one full of care
alas for a care-bearer!
    Others feel no grief
    bear no bitter heart
as those with a hidden love
    with a secret bond.
    There is not a horse
in a farmer's barnyard, in
    the best rectory
    that can draw my care
    to a fishless pool
    one quite without perch.
If it could to one with fish
they would all be filled with care
and the perch would be weighed down
with the cares that make me thin
with the griefs that blacken me.

    Many say of me
    and a lot think thus:
the crazy one has no care
the absent-minded no mind
and the simpleton no sense.

But I have more care
than a spruce has cones
a pine has needles
badlands have willows
the heath has heather.
Not even one knows
nor yet do nine understand
what is on this calloo's mind
what is in this swallow's head
what the calloo is thinking
the swallow keeps in her head.

The dove's heart is cold
feeding from the village ricks:
    mine is colder yet.
The calloo's spirits are low
swimming in chilly water
churning it below the ice
    mine are lower yet
    in a strange family
in another mother-kin.

There is no sister
    nor a mother's child
who I can tell my tale to
can speak my sorrow of mind.
    If I tell the smoke
the smoke will tell the doorpost
the doorpost will tell the yard
and the yard all the village;
a stranger will tell it fifth
a villager the tenth time.
If I speak to the fir shoots
chatter to the willow leaves
they will speak to nobody.

Better Unborn

Better for poor me
had I not been born, not grown
not had to come to this earth
not been suckled for the world
not tasted my mother's milk:
I should have died six nights old
been lost in my swaddling-band
needing but a span of cloth
a cubit of holy ground
    two words from the priest
three verses from the cantor
    one bong from the bell.

Grinding Song

I grind for my Jim
    twist for my crook-shank
but Jim does not grind for me
neither does the crook-shank twist
neither does the cripple rub.
The cripple's wife is well off
the halt of foot's has it made:
the cripple has fed me well
    the halt on fishes;
he is not led off to war
is not wanted in battle.
I myself, an old wife, grind,
    mouldy-eared, I pant:
for me no daughter-in-law
grinds, no son's wife turns the quern.

If the one I know came now
the one I've seen were in sight
I'd kiss him straight on the mouth
    I would stroke his chin.
But there's no sound of my dear!

At evening I long for him
when I go to bed 'tis worse
but at night 'tis bitterer
when I wake up 'tis sadder:
I grope at an empty space
    I grasp at a lie.
I would always get along
but the mornings are painful
when others are starting work
    or taking a rest
and to be alone at night
in bed without a husband
    not to have a mate
    who gives you a kiss
    who fingers your sides
    and tickles your loins!

Since there's no sound of my dear
knocking outside the cook-house
or chopping wood in the yard
    whittling at the gates
standing below the window –
come, poor love, to my cradle
step, sweetheart, into my bed!
But I'll not call out, oh no:
your nature will bring you, yes
blood will draw you to my side.
When you've come to my cradle
closer, closer, little bird
hither, hither, my treasure!

The Grave-Board

Man goes off to hunt a bear
with a grave-board on his back.
Man goes to cut a clearing
with a grave-board on his back.
Woman goes into labour
with a grave-board on her back.

The Muster

Now is the dead time on earth
in the air the time of tears
now no one knows anyone
mother does not know her child
the afflicted her womb-kin
where her likeness is walking
whether her flesh and blood strays
on the earth or on the sea
or wanders at war: the wolf
could be gulping down his bones
the eagle gathering them
the gull carrying them off.
Now on earth is the dead time
in the air the time of tears
now the lands support no crows –
lands no crows, the swamps no hares
   the field no small stones
   the grass no young bride
and the heath no growing thing.

   When deep autumn comes
and harsh winter trudges near
and aspens go grey with frost
and wretched birches dry out
and leaves fall from the alder
then to boys comes burning pain
heartbreak to those who bore them
grief comes to those with caps on
tears to those with helmets on:
boys begin to be picked for
a great war against the Swede
a fierce fire against the Turk
a battle against the Dane.

There upon the ground are heads
   like rocks upon shores
   upon rocky shores
there upon the ground is hair
like grass in a meadow, in

a grassy meadow
and there are ears there
like leaves of a birch
and there are eyes there
like so many blackcurrants
and there are leg bones
like treestumps in a clearing
and there are fingers
like shoots in a swamp
there below the town
in the troop below the town
clash of sword and crash of gun
and jingle of golden spur
and rattle of iron chain
there is blood up to the waist
and fog level with the leg
wheels rolling in blood
drums howling in gore.

Epilogue

Of what use are we singers
what good we cuckoo-callers
if no fire spurts from our mouths
no brand from beneath our tongues
and no smoke after our words!

ANONYMOUS

A Lament for Booze,
a Song for the Poor Thing's Death

Sorrow breaks the heart
grief crumbles the mind
when pipes are under torture
and all the pans in shackles
for booze has been put to death
and been lost the handsome drink
once among the crowd a joy
nourishment among the folk
good in the court of lords, good
in the house of farmers too
the best among everyone.
It consoled sorrowful minds
   cheered up the tearful;
it bestowed sense, gave a tongue
   it brought lively speech
   cooled the excited
   excited the cool
and what's more, it cleverly
made friends into enemies
and enemies into friends.

Alas for you, darling booze!
Who got you into trouble
   who had you hounded
when you had done nothing wrong
had committed no offence?
Alas for you, darling booze
   always to be missed
since you trod the ways of death
   drew close to your end
came to the brink of the grave!
Neither I nor any one
of my companions set you
on the paths of punishment
on the ways of correction:
you would be needed indoors

in the morning quite early
and late in the evening too
if at day's end we are bored
or at nightfall more fed up
or on waking more depressed
or as a blizzard hits us
in the face, boxes our ears.
Hear this as well, darling booze
old comrade and one of us:
don't die, whatever happens
though you have been taken ill
    crippled, subjected
    to many troubles –
a leg off, a wing broken
    good feathers scattered
flappers all over the place.
If you, one I know, came now,
you, one I've seen, were in sight
    I would kiss your mouth
    in a small goblet
    of gleaming silver.
Come back, little one I know,
be seen, little one I've seen
    before we must part
and the hour of death comes round:
you would surely be wished for
wanted with a great desire.

    Might the precious KING
the most merciful MASTER,
MAJESTY, LORD OF THE LAND
give a merciful command
    say a kindly word
    to set the pans free
    to their former state
    to hang down by their
    handle and drip drops
    so that we poor boys
in a poor land of the north
may at Savo's borders get
    a goblet to grasp
a stiffener before us!

TRADITIONAL

The Death of Elina

Klavus, Elina's mother, Elina,
Kirsti, Olovi, Jesus

       Elina the maid went to the shed
       a copper box in her hand
       a copper key in the box
         when she met Klavus:
Kl: 'Might you have a maid for sale
       has a girl been kept for me?'

M: 'No maid is sold on a hill
       and none traded on a farm:
         but rooms I have, one
       for coming, one for going.'

       That Klavus went to a room:
       Elina's five brothers sat
       each one at the table-head
         and each one stood up.

E: 'O my mother, my darling
       do not give me to Klavus!'

M: 'How do you know him?'
E: 'I know
       the stern one by his coming
       the swing of his noble foot.'

       With his sword he pushed the door
       open, with his scabbard shut:
Kl: 'My good woman, my darling
       have you got a maid for sale
       has a lass been kept for me?'

M: 'Small lasses I have
       and daughters half-grown.'

Kl: 'You have little Elina.'

M: 'Little Elina cannot
   take care of a big family
   look after a big stockyard
   nor set a hireling to work.'

Kl: 'See, I have the lass Kirsti
   to care for the big family
   to set the hireling to work
   look after the big stockyard.'

E: 'Yes, you have the lass Kirsti
   who will burn me in the fire
     and basely kill me.'

   But who else but the poor girl
   took the gifts and gave her hand
   walked at Klavus's manor
   hand in hand with him. The lass
   Kirsti peered through the window
     peeped in at the panes:
K: 'Oh! that somebody might come
     to spoil that union!'

   She went at once to Klavus:
K: 'O my Klavus, my darling
   Olovi is with my lady.'

Kl: 'O my Kirsti, my lassie
   if you can show to be true
   what you have put into words
   I'll burn Elina in fire
     then keep you in cloth.'

K: 'O my Klavus, my darling
   be as one going far off
   to Pohjanmaa assizes
   drive to the barn at Ammas
   round behind Little Meadows
   and then I'll show to be true
   what I have put into words.'

Kl: 'O my little Elina
    lay provisions in a bag
    put some butter in a box
      and a joint of ham
    and a bushel of hens' eggs
    for me to go far away
    to Pohjanmaa assizes.'

E: 'O my Klavus, my darling
    speak with half-words, another
    time give the latter half so
      that you may survive
    among the Pohja wizards.'

    That Klavus drove off
    drove to the barn at Ammas
    round behind Little Meadows:
    that Kirsti went to wash clothes.
    The lady came to the shore:
E: 'O my Kirsti, my lassie
      do not beat so hard
      my beautiful clothes:
      they were not got here
    but back in my mother's house.

    ...O my Kirsti, my lassie
      do not beat so hard
      my beautiful clothes:
      they were not got here
    but back in my mother's house.
    ...Do not beat, Kirsti, you whore
      quite so very hard
      my beautiful clothes:
    because they were not made here
    but back in my mother's house.'

K: 'But I do not count –
    I'm only a poor hireling:
    what a great mistress you are
    who have been with Olovi
    on the long-bearded one's breast!

O my lady, my darling
let us have a little feast
   as we used to have
when the master was away:
let us take the serfs off work
behind the wicked oxen.'

E: 'O my Kirsti, my lassie
   do just as you wish:
tap all the other barrels
   but don't tap the one
   which was brewed for me.'

And Kirsti thought of this trick:
   she tapped that one first.

E: 'O my Kirsti, my lassie
make my bed above the gate
   in the fair chamber:
   set out two pillows
   and two linen sheets
   two woollen covers.
...O my Kirsti, my lassie
you have not done as I said:
one pillow you have set out
   and one linen sheet
   one woollen cover.'

K: 'O my lady, my darling
Olovi called you to his room.'

E: 'But what am I to do there?'

She went there nevertheless.
Kirsti hurried after her
   and she locked nine locks
and shot a bolt for the tenth.
She went then to Ammas barn
round behind Little Meadows:
K: 'O my Klavus, my darling
I have just shown to be true
what I have put into words:
Olovi lay with my lady.'

Klavus rushed home, thrust a light
in a corner. Elina
thrust her finger through the pane:
E: 'O my Klavus, my darling
      do not lose your ring
   though you lose the ring's wearer.'

      Klavus drew his sword
      slashed the finger off.
   Elina prayed in the room:
      'Let all corners burn
   but let this one run water
   till I see my mother. Go
   hired man, to my mother's house
      tell her to come here!'

   The man came to Suomela:
O: 'My good woman, darling, my
   lady called you to Laukko.'

M: 'Woe is me, a wan woman:
   when I pull on my stockings
   they are always back to front.
      How is my daughter?'

O: 'Quite well, good woman.
   a cock is being scalded
   a hen is being plucked there
   for a tiny prince's feast.'

M: 'Woe is me, a wan woman:
   when I dress up in my dress
   it is always back to front.
   Woe is me, a wan woman.
      How is my daughter?'

O: 'Quite well, good woman.'

M: 'When I put on my kerchief
   it is always upside down.
      How is my daughter?'

O: 'Quite well, good woman.'

M: 'Ah, from Laukko smoke rises
   smoke from Klavus's manor.'

O: 'Lambs are being slaughtered there
   and pigs are being roasted
   for a tiny prince's feast.'

   The woman went on her knees
   before her own son-in-law:
M: 'O my Klavus, my darling
   take the boy out of the fire
   the sturdy wife from the flames:
   let her go to other lands
   to be ashamed of her deeds
     to cover her tracks.'

K: 'No, do not, my dear Klavus.
   Take a pan of bad flour, take
   a barrel of tar as well:
   perhaps she will burn better.
   Throw them here into the fire!'

M: 'O my darling Elina
   you might have curried favour
     with the harlot whore.'

E: 'There is not the slightest cause
   not even a needle-point.
     Let this corner burn
   now I have seen my mother!'

   Nothing henceforth prospered in Laukko:
   a stableful of horses
   a cowshedful of beasts died
   all died with straw in their mouths
     perished at their oats.
   Klavus Kurki, dreadful man
     both sat down and wept.

   Jesus as an old man walked:
J: 'Why do you weep, Klavus Kurki?'

Kl: 'There is good cause for weeping
    and trouble for bewailing:
    I have burnt, have burnt my spouse
    set fire to my good armful
    a stableful of horses
    a shedful of beasts has died
    all died with straw in their mouths
       perished at their oats.'

J: 'Do not weep, Klavus Kurki:
    I know Lady Elina.'

Kl: 'Where is Lady Elina?'

J: 'In the highest of heavens
      before six candles
    a golden book in her hand
    a little boy in her lap
    Olovi before the door.
    And I know Klavus Kurki.'

Kl: 'And where is Klavus Kurki?'

J: 'In the lowest hell:
    his spurs are just visible
      are faintly gleaming.
    And I know the whore Kirsti.'

Kl: 'And where is the whore Kirsti?'

J: 'In the lowest hell:
    her plaits are just visible.'

    That Klavus drove off.
    He packed his pipes in his bag
    played going over the marsh
    drove towards the open sea
    with Kirsti cur-like behind.
    And that was the young man's loss
    and the married fellow's too.

ARHIPPA PERTTUNEN

The Sampo

The Laplander, the slit-eyed
for ages harboured hatred
   for long bore ill-will
against old Väinämöinen:
he waited evenings, mornings
for Väinämöinen to come
for the man from Umento.
Then the old Väinämöinen
into his sledge flung himself
in his sleigh hoisted himself
with the straw-coloured stallion
with the pea-stalk-coloured horse
   drove rumbling away
upon the clear stretch of sea
   the open water.

The Laplander, the slit-eyed
on a day among others
one morning among many
spied a black speck on the sea
a bluish speck on the wave:
he took up his fiery bow
   from the fiery hut
   he flexed the bow taut
laid an arrow on the stock
   and chose the best shaft.
So then he uttered a word:
   'If my hand comes down
   let the arrow rise:
   if my hand comes up
   let the arrow fall.'
He shot the straw-hued stallion
from under Väinämöinen
and the pea-stalk-coloured horse
   through the collar-bone
   through the right shoulder
   under the left arm.

Then the old Väinämöinen
sank with fingers to the waves
turned with palms to the water:
there he wandered for six years
stopped there for seven summers
    wandered as a spruce
as a log from a pine tree
    in tears he drizzled
    he prayed to Ukko
and worshipped Pavannainen:

'Raise up, Ukko, a great wind
let the weather know no boundS
    raise lumps of black slime
to fall on the clear waters!'

Ukko raised up a great wind
let the weather know no bounds
    raised lumps of black slime
to fall on the clear waters.
He bore old Väinämöinen
    to dark Pohjola
to the side of a bright rock
the edge of a thick boulder.
    In tears he drizzled.

The gap-toothed crone of Pohjo
rose when it was quite early
quite early in the morning:
    quickly warmed her room
    cleaned all through the rooms
taking a broom to the floor
then she took the dust outside
    to the farthest field
and stopped at the rubbish-tip.
There she listened from six sides
    attended from eight:
she could hear a man weeping
could hear a hero wailing.
The sobs were no woman's sobs
nor were the sobs a child's sobs:
these were Väinämöinen's sobs
the wails of Untamoinen.

There, then the crone of Pohjo
dressed herself and decked herself
adorned her head prettily
splendidly adorned her head.
She went to Väinämöinen
she uttered a word, spoke thus:
'Why are you weeping, Väinö
why, Untamo, do you wail?'

The old Väinämöinen said:
'For this I weep all my life
    grieve throughout my days:
    I've swum to strange lands
    to quite unknown doors.'

So the crone of Pohjo said:
'So what will you give me, if
I take you to your own lands
there to hear your own cockcrow
    far from these strange lands
    these quite unknown doors?'

The old Väinämöinen said:
'Well, what do you ask of me?'

So the crone of Pohjo said:
'If you shaped a new Sampo
worked a brightly-worked cover
from one feather of a swan
from one piece of a distaff
    one snippet of wool
the milk of a barren cow
    from one barley-grain.'

The old Väinämöinen said:
'I myself cannot hammer
nor can I work a cover.
I'll get smith Ilmorinen:
he is the most skilled craftsman
he knows how to work covers.'

At that the crone of Pohjo
delivered the man from death
took up old Väinämöinen
    brought him to her home:
gave the man food, gave him drink
    nursed him back from death
she set a stallion running
a flaxen-maned one moving
    from dark Pohjola
from the gloomy arctic sea
from the man-eating village
the village that drowns heroes.

    When he got back home
    he went to the smith.
He uttered a word, spoke thus:
    'Smith Ilmorinen
my kinsman, my mother's child!
Set out to bring back a maid
to look for a plaited head
    from dark Pohjola:
now a maiden has been wooed
a plaited head bargained for.'

Then the smith Ilmorinen
    washed, cleaned himself up
from the autumn-hued charcoal
from the winter-hued forge-grime
he drew broadcloth about him
buckled on his armoured belt
into his sledge flung himself
into his sleigh stirred himself
brought the lash down on his horse
clouted with the beaded whip:
the stallion ran, the road sped
    to dark Pohjola
to the gloomy arctic sea
to the man-eating village
the village that drowns heroes.

When he got to Pohjola
the gap-toothed crone of Pohjo
set him to shape the Sampo
to work the bright-worked cover
from one feather of a swan
    from one barley-grain
    one snippet of wool
the milk of a barren cow
from one piece of a distaff.

Then the smith Ilmorinen
by day he built the Sampo
and by night courted the maid:
then the smith Ilmorinen
    fashioned the Sampo
brightly worked the bright-covered
but the maid was not courted.

The new Sampo was grinding
the bright-covered was rocking:
it ground a binful at dusk
ground a binful for eating
ground a binful for selling
a third for storing away.

The crone of Pohjo was charmed
and she gave her own daughtcr
to the smith Ilmorinen
to be his wife for ever
be a hen under his arm
    to place his pillow
to be always on her feet.

Then the smith Ilmorinen
as he came towards his home
    cuckoos were calling
on the prow of the bright sleigh
    squirrels ran about
    on the maple shafts
    black grouse were cooing
on the collar-bow of elm.

The smith Ilmorinen's hand
was in a bright-worked mitten
the other on the maid's breasts
his foot in a German boot
the other between her thighs
as he came from Pohjola.

When he arrived home
the old Väinämöinen went
to the smith Ilmorinen
and asked him, spoke up:
'Brother, smith Ilmorinen
my kinsman, my mother's child!
Have you made the new Sampo
brightly worked the bright-covered?'

The smith Ilmorinen said:
'I have shaped the new Sampo
from milk of a barren cow
one snippet of wool
from one piece of a distaff
from one barley-grain.'
The old Väinämöinen said:
'Has it ground, the new Sampo
the bright-covered been rocking?'

The smith Ilmorinen said:
'It has ground, the new Sampo
the bright-covered been rocking:
it ground a binful at dusk
ground a binful for eating
ground a binful for selling
a third for storing away.'

Then the old Väinämöinen
when he understood this news
set about building his ship
launched his ship out on the sea
uttered a word, speaking thus:
'Who is there among these men
with the old Väinämöinen? —
Iku Tiera, Niera's son
foremost of my friends.'

He hoisted his masts
like a pine-clump on a hill
he sailed out on the blue sea
leaning on his curved paddle
he sailed a day, another:
Pohjola's gates were in sight
the evil hinges shining
the evil doorways squealing.

He fumbled in his pocket
then Väinämöinen groped
    about in his purse
    took out sleeping-darts
sent the wicked folk to sleep
oppressed the pagan people.
He sailed out on the blue sea
    to dark Pohjola.

He uttered a word, spoke thus:
'Iku Tiera, Niera's son
    foremost of my friends
go and seize the Sampo, you,
carry off the bright-covered!'

Iku Tiera, Niera's son
    quick to take orders
    easy to persuade
went off to seize the Sampo
carry off the bright-covered
but the Sampo would not move
the bright-covered would not shift:
its roots were rooted in earth.

The old Väinämöinen went
himself to seize the Sampo
carry off the bright-covered
but the Sampo would not move:
its roots were rooted in earth.
Then the old Väinämöinen
ploughed the roots of the Sampo
with a hundred-hornèd ox
a thousand-headed sea-worm
bore the Sampo to his boat
and placed it in his vessel.

He hoisted his mast
he sailed out on the blue sea
he sailed a day, another
    so on the third day
an ant, a ballocking boy
pissed on the leg of a crane
    in dark Pohjola.
The crane let out a great squawk
screeched out in an evil tone:
the whole of Pohjola woke
the evil realm was awake.

The gap-toothed crone of Pohjo
groped about for her Sampo:
'The Sampo has been removed
the bright-covered carried off!'
She built the craft of Pohjo –
a hundred men to punt it
a hundred fellows to oars
a hundred men armed with swords
a hundred men for shooting:
she sailed out on the blue sea.

Iku Tiera, Niera's son
uttered a word, speaking thus:
'O you old Väinämöinen
    sing, you well-born man
now you've got the good Sampo
now you've trodden the good road!'

The old Väinämöinen said:
'It is too early to cheer
    still too soon to sing:
Pohjola's gates are in sight
the evil hinges glitter
and the evil portals squeal.
If our own doors were in sight
our own portals were squealing
then it would be right to sing
and fitting to make merry.'

He said in these words
did the old Väinämöinen:
'Foremost of my friends
climb up now to the mast-tip
   clamber up the mast
look eastward, look to the west
look along Pohjo's coastline!'

Iku Tiera, Niera's son
   quick to take orders
   easy to persuade
climbed up then to the mast-tip
   clambered up the mast
looked eastward, looked to the west
looked along Pohjo's coastline
   and said in these words:
'Now Pohjo's craft is coming
a hundred rowlocks chopping –
a hundred men punting it
a hundred fellows at oars
a hundred men armed with swords
a hundred more for shooting.'

Then the old Väinämöinen
   saw his doom coming
his day of distress dawning:
he fumbled in his pocket
he groped about in his purse
found a tiny piece of flint
a little scrap of tinder
pitched them right into the sea
cast them in the arctic sea
straight over his right shoulder
   under his left arm.
He himself uttered these words:
'A crag was formed in the sea
a hidden isle spirited
stretching eastward for ever
   westward without end
on and on to Pohjola
upon which craft would be jammed
   and boats would be caught!'
And so Pohjo's craft was jammed
the strong-rowlocked boat was split.

The gap-toothed crone of Pohjo
rose on a skylark's pinions
on a bunting's wings went up
she beat bath-whisks into wings
upon an eagle's wing-bones:
    she flew, she fluttered
upon the clear stretch of sea
    the open water.
    She glided, hovered
to Väinämöinen's mast-head:
the craft's bow began to sink
the ship to smash to pieces.

So old Väinämöinen said:
'Iku Tiera, Niera's son
    foremost of my friends
    take up your own sword
    now in your right hand
from its scabbard on your left:
smite the eagle on the claws
the wyvern upon the toes!'

Iku Tiera, Niera's son
    took up his own sword
    took in his right hand
from its scabbard on his left
smote the eagle on the claws
the wyvern upon the toes
but he did not cut the hide
nor take off the outer skin.
He struck once, he struck again
soon a third time he laid waste:
he left no mark on the hide
he took off no outer skin.

Old Väinämöinen himself
raised a paddle from the sea
    his oar from the waves
smote the eagle on the claws
the wyvern upon the toes.
One nameless finger was left
    to seize the Sampo
carry off the bright-covered.

Then the old Väinämöinen
   took up his own sword
   took in his right hand
from its scabbard on his left.
Then he shattered the Sampo
the bright-covered brightly flashed
upon the clear stretch of sea
   the open water.
   And the wind lulled them
and the soft breeze shifted them
   about the blue sea:
washed all the other pieces
   up on the seashore
   up on the sea-slush.
The gap-toothed crone of Pohjo
carried the cover home, the
handle to the cold village
bore with her nameless finger
   bore with her left toe.

The Messiah

   Always other things
   are recalled, never
   the great killing of
   God, the Lord's harsh death
how the Creator was killed
and the Almighty destroyed
   with a hundred spears
   a thousand sword-points
   no greater number
   no smaller number:
a horse stood on the spearhead
a colt ran along the shaft
a barren cow on the sleeve
a cat mewed in the peg-place
a pig where the haft-joint was.

When the Creator was killed
and the Almighty destroyed
the rocks were heaped under him
rocks under, the slabs on top
the gravel against the heart.

So the sun, creature of God
flew as a headless chicken
as one cut down, its wing whirred
to the Creator's grave-side.
   In tears it drizzled:
'Rise, O Creator, from death
O Lord, awake from the grave
   or I too will come
   to die beside you
   to perish with you!'

And so our great Creator
uttered a word, speaking thus:
'There is no rising from here
as there is hoping from there:
the rocks are heaped under me
the gravel against the heart.
   Sun, creature of God
fly as a headless chicken
as one cut down, whirr your wing
   to where you once were
   to your place of old!
Blaze for one moment sultry
another dimly swelter
for a third with your whole disc
send the wicked crowd to sleep
oppress the pagan people
slump the young on their arrows
the old over their spear-hafts!'

So the sun, creature of God
   both flew and made haste
   to where it once was
   to its place of old:
blazed for one moment sultry
another dimly sweltered

for a third with its whole disc
slumped the young on their arrows
the old over their spear-hafts.

And so our great Creator
the Creator rose from death
and then the rocks sang with tongues
the boulders chattered with words
the rivers stirred, the lakes shook
the copper mountains trembled.

The Creator rose from death
the Lord awoke from the grave
went as poor man to the forge
as beggar to the cellar:
there the iron-men hammered
the smiths of Hiisi pounded.
He uttered a word, spoke thus:
'What do the iron-men pound
the smiths of Hiisi hammer?'

The cruellest of the Jews
the worst of the evil boys
basest of father's sons said:
'Well now, you have eyes as big
    eyelashes as long
    as yesterday's god
whom we buried in the earth
    heaped the rocks on top
rocks under, the rocks on top
the gravel against the heart.'

And the great Creator said
    and the pure God spoke:
'This is why I have big eyes
why I have long eyelashes:
long I watched the Creator's
mouth, the beard of who bites off,
the jaws of who grinds and sifts.'

The cruellest of the Jews
worst of the evil boys said:

'That was the worst thing I did
I did not think to measure
how long the Creator's beard
   how long and how thick
   and how wide across
so I cannot hammer that.'

So the great Creator said
   and the pure God spoke:
'The Creator's neck is long
   as long and as thick
   and as wide across
   as your own neck is.'

The cruellest of the Jews
worst of the evil boys said:
   'My hand will not turn
   nor is my finger
   fit to measure it.'

And the great Creator said:
   'My hand would turn it
   my finger would be
   fit to measure it.'

The cruellest of the Jews said:
'If I let it be measured
do not lock me in a lock
nor press on a buckle-pin:
the lock is not loosed with hands
the bolts not eased with fingers.
   No key has been made:
only the lock has been formed.'

Then he let it be measured.
And so our great Creator
   and so our Lord God
then locked him into the lock
pressed him on the buckle-pin.
So then he put into words:

'Stay in there, scoundrel
    howl in there, accurst
in the evil you have done
in the fetters you have made
as long as the moon, the sun
the day are fair to look on!'

He bore the end to the rock
himself put this into words:
    'From this day forward
fire is to light the heavens
water to temper iron!'

He hardened rock with a shout
tempered iron with a roar.

FRANS MICHAEL FRANZÉN

The Human Face

> *The human face divine*
> MILTON

The moment when old Time's sixth day
had cast its purple veil away
    from off the cedar grove
the gold-winged butterfly flew o'er
the stream towards the rosy bower
    and kissed it out of love.

The pearl shone in the water bright
and the swan's sails were glittering white
    upon the sheltered sound;
with grapes the vine was glowing red
and the dove, tender, blameless, played
    in the calm all around.

And yet the highest loveliness
nature still lacks, the world is less,
    uncrowned creation lies
till man out of the dust, the night
raises his face towards the light
    and then opens his eyes.

The snow turned pale upon the fells,
the daybreak sank behind the hills
    in deepest darkness furled;
the star that twinkled on day's brow
so handsomely will not stay now
    to shine upon the world.

The beasts in homage turned their gaze
away, whose eyes they used to raise
    to see the day run by,
where winsomeness and love once beamed,
where amid sorrow's tears once gleamed
    hope that would never die.

The angels stand beneath a spell,
behold a beauty that can tell,
    and see the Lord the while:
upon his work the Lord has set
his Seal, reflected sees in it
    his likeness, with a smile.

All you who cry out: There is nothing
within that has the flesh for clothing,
    all is but dust, no more –
fools! Only step beside a pool,
look at your face and silent fall,
    and then cover it o'er.

Look at the ancient Sage's brow:
a likeness of the truth will show
    that gives the ages light.
Look at the Hero's flashing eye
and see a lightning from on high
    that sets the worlds aright.

What of the fair, the sweet, the good?
Lift up my Selma's morning hood
    that hides her rosy cheek:
see how her eye is downcast, shy,
how in the wind her dark locks fly
    free – there is what you seek.

Or when she flees in secret, follow
her to a cabin in a hollow,
    led by the voice of need:
see there her visage as she plays
with the small ones, how by her gaze
    the sick are comforted.

A glimpse of heaven here in nature!
An angel-presence in a creature!
    O human face! do you
merely adorn mortality?
Will you not in eternity
    be tearful, smiling too?

Oh yes! the angels will be stirred
by Selma's face when they have heard
   her voice among them trill.
Selma! in heaven's palaces
and in the dales of paradise
   I may behold you still!

The Ages of Life

O carefree innocence! with a smile you wake
and gaze at heaven, gaze with such heartfelt joy
      on morning's first glow: *Child!* so happy
   still you are made by a moment's brightness.

The world shines pure: make haste to look all around,
you fiery *Youngster*. Far off you hear the call
      of nymphs at play in myrtle hollows,
   or of a steep where a temple glitters.

O blessed! you who early have sown your field
and crown your noon now, *Man!* with the fruit of stems
      you planted for yourself: meanwhile some
   madman is knocking at fortune's doorway.

Ah, heavy, dark that path in the gathering dusk
across the heath home. Phantoms and robbers fill
      with fear the *Old Man's* failing eyes that
   soon in the longest of nights are closing.

Sit firm upon your threshold and still rejoice
at evening's last glow. Though it is cloudy, look:
      one star is twinkling past the cloud-bank
   while you are bidding the wanderer welcome.

In friendship share your bread with the weary one,
put out the lamp in silence and sleep in peace
      until a morning with no evening
   wakes you anew to eternal springtime.

MATRO

The Hanged Maid

The girl Anni, matchless girl
went to the wood for bath-whisks
to the thicket for bath-whisks:
broke off one for her father
another for her mother
   a third she gathered
for her youngest brother, the
   best in the family.

Osmonen slipped from the dell
Kalevainen from the clearing:
   'Grow, maid, to please me
not the other young people
   the fair young people:
grow in narrow, in neat things
grow tall in dresses of cloth.'

The girl Anni, matchless girl
   went weeping homeward
   wailing to the farm.

Father was at the window
was whittling an axe-handle:
'Why do you weep, Anni girl?'

'The cross has slipped from my breast
the ring slipped from my finger
my trinkets off my belt's end
   the beads from my eyes
the gold tassels from my brows.'

Her brothers in the gateway
were adorning a bright sleigh
were building a box-sledge: 'Why
do you weep, sister Anni?'

'There is cause for my weeping:
the cross has slipped from my breast.'

The girl Anni, matchless girl...

Her sisters upon the floor
were weaving a belt of gold
working one of silver: 'Why
do you weep, sister Anni
sister Anni, matchless one?'

'The cross has slipped from my breast
the ring slipped from my finger
my trinkets off my belt's end.'

Mother on the shed step was
washing butter in a pail:
'Why do you weep, Anni girl
you girl Anni, matchless girl?'

'I went to the wood for whisks
to the thicket for bath-whisks
broke off one for my father.
Osmonen called from the dale
Kalevainen from the clearing:
    "Grow, maid, to please me
not the other young people
    the fair young people:
grow in narrow, in neat things." '

'You girl Anni, matchless girl
    don't weep, Anni girl.
Three are the sheds on the hill.
Step to the shed on the hill
    open the best shed:
there eat butter for a year
and grow plumper than others
    another year, pork
    and a third, fish pies.
    Stand trunk upon trunk
    case on top of case:
    open the best trunk
make the bright lid slam open
    put on the best things
the most gorgeous on your breasts.'

The girl Anni, matchless maid
stepped to the shed on the hill
    opened the worst shed
became prettier than others
became plumper than others
    opened the worst trunk
    found six golden belts
    eight swaddling-girdles
strangled herself with the belts
choked herself with the girdles
    she staggered, she slumped
hanged herself with her own thread:
then she dropped upon the case
    fell on the trunk-lid.

Her mother came to the shed
    when three years had passed:
the girl Anni was no more.

'Roll, a tear, roll, another
let my brimming waters roll
    on my fine skirt-hems
    on my gorgeous breasts
roll, a tear, roll, another
    on my silk belt-ends
roll, a tear, roll, another
    on my silk stockings
    lower still than that
    on my fine skirt-hems
    lower still than that
    upon my fair heels
the heels of my golden shoes
roll, a tear, roll, another
    lower still than that
to the earth-mothers below
to the earth for the earth's good.'

    Now three rivers came
and a fiery river came
    from one maiden's tears
    three birches were bred

on the bank of each river
   three cuckoos were bred
out of one person's weeping.

   The third called *love, love*
   to the nameless child
   the first called *joy, joy*
   to the joyless child
   the second *love, love*
   to the loveless child
   the third called *joy, joy*
to the child with no father.

JAAKKO JUTEINI

A Song in Finland

We too are worthy folk
on Finland's mighty soil
whose crops do not delight
the man who does not toil:
bread for the ploughman grows
and labour earns repose.

The son of Finland tills
and all his strength he wields
subduing wilderness
to turn it into fields:
in peace he takes delight
in war knows how to fight.

On paths of learning too
our Finnish scholars throng
and many sing and play
anew the ancient song:
enlightenment and reason
here flourish in their season.

On Finland's daughter's cheeks
the blood bursts into flower:
grey frost cannot remain
nor the cold overpower
the lass whose ways are mild
whose heart is never wild.

On the Apple

Women speaking of the life
    of the first Eve
heap a load of blame on her
that the wretched mother longed
    for an apple
and devoutly fingered it;
but our daughters for themselves
    do not study
their behaviour carefully:
many gather in cupped hands
    by the fistful
boughs and apples even now.

A Child's Song to a Widow

Do not weep, dear mother
do not weep, my dear
even though my father
is no longer here.

Do not dwell on sorrow:
there the sky is bright.
I will ward off hunger,
grief will lose its might.

Soon this childish body
will have all its power
and one day a man's strength
in its arm will flower.

Let a little time pass,
I will smooth your brow:
bread will grow in plenty
when I come to plough.

PIETARI MAKKONEN

A Glad Song about the Growth
of the Finnish Tongue

Where was Finland's maiden born
where did the shy child grow up
where did she learn her lessons
   pick up special words
when with her tongue she was not
allowed in a drawing-room
   nor taught lessons, nor
   given instruction?
That's why never in this world
did she hobnob with the great
   nor in her day make
   friends with the highest:
she walked in poor villages
   in humble abodes
in the cabins of peasants
   the yards of ploughmen.
If she ever got to court
   she was not let in
but could only tread the yard
and beside the wall shiver;
nor did she manage a pen
   get used to a quill
nor have access to the law
   nor come to judgement.

So she was of no account
standing behind people's backs
   like a poor beggar
an orphan child at the door;
the great tongues could not take her
the tongues of power as their peer
   nor did they give help
for teaching the orphan child.
   From grief her figure
   became quite wasted;
with a threadbare coat on her

of thoroughly old homespun
she felt foolish as to words
and simple as to learning.

That's how she walked all the time
   living by her wits
then the lords in Helsinki
   saw a use for her
started being nice to her.
From that sprang a great Society
a praiseworthy Book Society
   that starts – for a start –
by teaching the orphan child:
they wipe the dirt from her eyes
from her neck they cleaned the muck
   and made her ears fair
adorned them with golden chains
   washed her all over
   whitened her with soap
   brushed her hair handsome
   till it was all curls;
her breasts they made fair with flowers
the best ones from a palm tree,
put on her a linen shirt
a white one of choicest flax;
the cape was Karelian
the tunic got from Savo
from Kemi the shoes were brought
and the stockings from Kainuu.
They put her to school at home,
to their lessons they set her:
one guided her in words, one
instructed her in music.

   Then the fair maid grew
Finland's lassie rose, her mouth
is as with a feather formed;
on her lips honey glistens
   her face fair, graceful
   blooming like a rose
   her eyes shining blue

as forget-me-nots and wide;
by nature she is cheerful
   her breast full of love.

And now in a drawing-room
   in a fair chamber
   properly herself
she can stand among the great
with some fine books in her hand
and she sings a song of love
like a bird in a grove, like
a ringdove in the forest:
now she measures up to the
damsels of renowned Sweden.
And the lords in Helsinki
all look upon her with joy
and the young unmarried lords
   compete to win her.

SIMANA SISSONEN

Lemminkäinen

Now, Väinölä held a feast
and Sinivermo revels:
masters, pastors were bidden
the crippled, the lame were asked
the crippled were rowed in boats
the lame driven on horseback
all Christian people were asked
but Lemminkäinen was not.
Lemminkäin, he the blackguard
enjoyed his only sister
and ruined his mother's child.

Wanton Lemminkäinen said
said to his only father
said to his darling mother:
'I'm off to Väinölä's feast.'

Father banned, mother said no:
    'Don't go, my offspring
to that feast at Väinölä!
    There are three harsh deaths:
a pond lies across the road
brimming over with hot rocks
    with boulders on fire.'

Wanton Lemminkäinen said:
'A father's knowledge is good:
my own knowledge is better.
Yes, I shall find a way out:
I'm off as I intended
to that feast at Väinölä
to Sinivermo's revels.

Father banned, mother said no
    'Don't go, my offspring!
A worm lies across the road
longer than the standing trees
thicker than the lane's pillar.'

Wanton Lemminkäinen said:
'A father's knowledge is good
my own knowledge is better.
Yes, I shall find a way out:
I shall sing the worm aside.
That's how I'll deal with that one.'

Wanton Lemminkäinen said:
'Dear father, my only one
quickly bring my war-stallion!
I'm off as I intended
to that feast at Väinölä
to Sinivermo's revels.'

Father banned, mother said no:
    'Don't go, my offspring!
There is a third, harsher death:
a wolf is bridled ready
and bears in iron fetters
    stand across the steps.'

Wanton Lemminkäinen said:
'A father's knowledge is good:
my own knowledge is better.
Yes, I shall find a way out:
I shall sing a flock of sheep
a cluster of curly-wools
into the iron wolves' mouths
in the iron bear's fetters.
That's how I'll deal with that one.'

Wanton Lemminkäinen said:
'Dear father, my only one
dear mother, my darling one!
I'm off as I intended
dear mother, my darling one:
    bring my battledress!'
She quickly brought his war-gear.

Wanton Lemminkäinen said:
'Quickly bring me, my father
that old war-stallion of mine
get my battle-colt ready!'

His father, his only one
quickly brought his war-stallion
got his battle-colt ready
for his son, his only one
leaving for Väinölä's feast.

Wanton Lemminkäinen left
for that feast at Väinölä:
'twas wanton Lemminkäinen
flung his brush against the wall.
Wanton Lemminkäinen said:
'When the brush is oozing blood
then Lemminkäinen is lost
things look black for the bad boy
at that feast at Väinölä
at Sinivermo's revels.'

And still his mother said no:
    'Don't go, my offspring!
Over there you will be sung
you'll be sung, you'll be sentenced
into Tuoni's black river
Manala's eternal stream
with your nails on a cold rock
with your teeth in a wet log
to weep everlastingly
    and wail for ever.'

Wanton Lemminkäinen left
and he drove a little way
he made tracks a short distance.
A pond lay across the road
brimming over with hot rocks
    with boulders on fire:
'twas wanton Lemminkäinen
    cooled the pond to ice
and froze the water to frost.
That's how he dealt with that one.

And he drove a little way.
A worm lay across the road
longer than the standing trees
thicker than the lane's pillar:

'twas wanton Lemminkäinen
    sang the worm aside
whose throat was boiling with fire.
That's how he dealt with that one.

'Twas wanton Lemminkäinen
drove into Väinölä's yards
    to those sloping yards
into the level paddocks.
There were wolves bridled ready
and bears in iron fetters
    stood across the steps
and they went to attack him:
'twas wanton Lemminkäinen
    sang a flock of sheep
a cluster of curly-wools
into the iron wolves' mouths
in the iron bear's fetters.
That's how he dealt with that one.

He uttered the moment he
    came to that great house
he arrived at Väinölä:
'Greetings, for I have come here!'

Old Väinämöinen uttered:
'Greetings to who shouts greetings!
Hail, wanton Lemminkäinen:
you have not been invited.'

Wanton Lemminkäinen said:
'A wretch comes at a summons:
a good man leaps up without.'

Wanton Lemminkäinen said:
'Is there room in a corner
for the guest who is coming
for the one on his way in?
Are there nails for bright mittens
a stall where a horse may stay
barley for a horse to munch
beer for a hero to drink?'

Old Väinämöinen uttered:
'There is no room for you here
for the guest who is coming
and there are no nails for bright mittens
there is no stall where a horse may stay
and no barley for a horse to munch
and no beer for a hero to drink:
by the door, beneath the beam
in the space between two pots
where three hooks turn to and fro
if you will behave inside.'

Wanton Lemminkäinen said:
'In the old days my father
was not by the door, beneath the beam
nor was my noble parent
in the space between two pots
where three hooks turn to and fro:
there was room in a corner
there were nails for bright mittens
there were walls to size up swords
a stall where a horse might stay
barley for a horse to munch
beer for a hero to drink –
so why is there not for me
as there was for my father?'

Old Väinämöinen uttered:
'You're wanton Lemminkäinen
you are the worst of blackguards
you ruined your mother's child
enjoyed your only sister:
    go, scoundrel, to hell
bad boy, flee to your country
away from all Christian folk!'

Old Väinämöinen uttered:
'If you don't do as you're told...'
Lemminkäinen paid no heed.

The ancient Väinämöinen
the everlasting wise man
son of doughty days, it was
he who sang Lemminkäinen

damned the son of Kaleva
into Tuoni's black river
Manala's eternal stream
where trees topple uprooted
    grasses fall headlong
with his nails on a cold rock
with his teeth in a wet log
to weep everlastingly
    and wail for ever.
Then Lemminkäinen was lost
things looked black for the bad boy.

The brush started oozing blood.
Lemminkäinen's mother said:
'Now Lemminkäinen is lost
things look black for the bad boy
when the brush is oozing blood.'

Lemminkäinen's mother went
away in search of her son
to that feast at Väinölä
to Sinivermo's revels:
where logs were across the road
    she turned them aside
where there were rocks on the road
moved them all to the roadside.

Lemminkäinen's mother said
    asked questions, spoke up:
'Hail, old Väinämöinen: where
have you sung Lemminkäinen
damned the son of Kaleva?'

Old Väinämöinen uttered:
'I don't know your son, harlot
nor, bitch, do I know your fruit.'

Lemminkäinen's mother said:
'Hullo, old Väinämöinen:
if you don't tell of my son
where you've sung, where sentenced him
damned the son of Kaleva
if you don't tell of my son
the new threshing-house doors I'll
break down, smash the sky's hinges.'

Väinämöinen grew worried
the bearded hero was pained.
Old Väinämöinen uttered:
'I have sung Lemminkäinen
into Tuoni's black river
damned the son of Kaleva
where trees topple uprooted
    grasses fall headlong
with his nails on a cold rock
with his teeth in a wet log
to weep everlastingly
    and wail for ever.'

'Twas Lemminkäinen's mother
flew to Tuonela's river
Manala's eternal stream:
    gliding, hovering
    she searched for her son
down in Tuoni's black river
but she did not find her son.
'Twas Lemminkäinen's mother
made a rake out of iron
fitted it with copper teeth
and raked with it for her son
along Tuonela's river:
now Lemminkäinen was caught
upon the copper rake's teeth
caught by his nameless finger.

'Twas Lemminkäinen's mother
    asked questions, spoke up:
'Will a man still come of you
a new hero be active?'

'There's no man in the one gone
no hero in the one drowned:
down there is this heart of mine
beside a blue rock, within
the liver-coloured belly.
Bitter now are my shoulders
rotten is my mound of flesh
down in Tuoni's black river
Manala's eternal stream

for I have been long in the grim place
ages in the chill water
with my nails on a cold rock
with my teeth in a wet log:
bitter there are my shoulders
rotten is my mound of flesh.'

Wanton Lemminkäinen said:
'Never may my kinsmen put
the blame on who is blameless
the guilt on who is guiltless:
the wages are badly paid
down in Tuoni's black river
Manala's eternal stream
where trees topple uprooted
      grasses fall headlong.'

Wanton Lemminkäinen said:
'Never may earthly people
nor ever may my kinsmen
my excellent tribesmen put
the blame on who is blameless
the guilt on who is guiltless:
here is surely room for you
down in Tuoni's black river
Manala's eternal stream.
Room is sure, bed is ready
      a bed of hot rocks
      of boulders on fire
a cover laid on the bed
      of the earth's black worms
      and of stabbing snakes.'

And still Lemminkäinen said:
'Room is sure, the place is bad
in the hands of death the harsh.
My mother, my only one
not of me will a man come
of father's son no hero:
there's no man in the one gone
nor in one who is quite lost.'

ABRAHAM POPPIUS

The Sparrow

'Sparrow, lackaday!
Every winter's day
Round the house you flutter to and fro.
If you had the will
You would flee the chill
Like the swallow many moons ago.

'High upon the gable
You hold that your fable
Is the kind for which all creatures long;
But no man will flatter
Your twittering chatter
By referring to it as a song.'

Then the sparrow sang
As it lulled its young,
From a rowan chirped to me the reason
Why it would not fly
Nor could go away
Like the lark, the partridge in their season:

'My father of late
Went to seek a mate –
Though grey, he flew headlong on his quest!
He did not live long
But he left a throng;
I was at the bottom of the nest.

'I was hardly fledged
When the first cranes edged
(As they must) towards a distant land
Though there still as much
Grain they did not touch
Spread on hurdles, scattered on the ground.

'I yelled after them:
"Kindly take your time –
Such a chance to feed does not come twice!"
     But below the feast
     The cold and the frost
Had converted lake and land to ice.

'If I then had known
     How winter brings down
Everything the earth has dared to raise,
     Yes, I would have flown
     With others (a groan
'Twould have cost) beyond the ocean's ways.

'But when the sun shines
     Pouring its gold coins
Over snowdrifts, over sea and land,
     When winter is done
     And spring can get on,
That is when I have a change of mind.

'I go wooing, burn,
     Make a bargain, yearn
For the one I want to share my life;
     Soon the heavenly
     Father will supply
Extra work for me and for my wife.

'First of all we build
     A nest, to be filled
Through the summer with our little elves;
     Parents get no rest
     In a hungry nest
Or outside, when chicks fend for themselves.

'Now I have a place
     Within a roof-space,
So I am not lost when summer leaves;
     Unless the Lord will,
     No creature may kill
Even a sparrow underneath the eaves.'

KAARLE AKSELI GOTTLUND

The Great Fire of Turku
4-5 September 1827

Fire has reduced our Turku to a ruin,
wild flame has done it damage beyond cost:
churches, great houses, towers and city walls –
    all has been lost.

The wind rose, flung itself into the midst,
fanning the flames, to fury lewdly yielding
and the flare flew like devils, fluttering from
    building to building.

What spread like a forest fire from corner to corner,
sucked into its mouth even the greatest abode,
what gnawed at stone, what took a bite at wood was
    the wrath of God.

Ghastly it was to gaze upon vain labour:
the pitiless great terror of the town,
the fairest streets were ashes, totally
    to dust brought down.

And O how terrible that autumn night!
Victims lamented, called out, said their prayers,
their weeping, screaming, moaning rang out all
    along the shores.

And many hundreds had nowhere to go:
only a field even the old folk found
and thousands in their sorrow had to sleep
    on the icy ground.

Lord who exaltest some and must put down
others, thy gift and penalty are near:
the best of landowners, the worst of tenants
    were sleeping here.

Serfs and their lords were not distinguished now:
the hounded and the hated with each other
made peace, the humble and the proud were all
        thrown here together.

Aura, our river that brought knowledge, wisdom
enlightening the land to advance our learning,
and books that told again of ancient things –
        all these were burning.

Records of Council, secrets of the Law
all crumbled and forthwith to ashes fell:
the fire permitted refuge to no man.
        What hours of hell!

Even the famous church, biggest in Finland
(O great cathedral, what days did you see
when fire wrought havoc long ago!) is now
        razed utterly.

Its very tower once built to be so fair
whose copper harmony has long been heard*
and men thought old and permanent, in flames
        has disappeared.

Joy turns to grief so soon. O memories!
Alas for blessed times! We are bereft
of everything: beyond an empty space
        nothing is left.

*As we recall, the bell-ringer rang his bell here during the hellish fire
until he turned black while the tower burnt (author's note).

ELIAS LÖNNROT

Elegy

Chance has driven a wretch to wander far from his homeland
    That he may study abroad places where foreigners live.
Things are different here and nothing resembles the home place,
    Not a familiar soul for the exchange of a word.
Foreign the tongue and strange is the life and strange are the manners,
    All of them hard to endure, all of them grim to behold.
When I was living at home, I remember, I studied the Ancients:
    Fleeting then were the days, vanishing like any smoke –
Fleeting then were the days and the nights were past in a moment;
    Now my days drag on, long are the days and the nights.
Now as I look at the sun I am thinking over and over:
    O if only I might see it resplendent at home,
Or when the Great Bear shines at night with a host of its comrades –
    These as well I would see rather if I were at home.
Therefore neither the sun nor the Great Bear give of their beauty,
    Nor do the other stars, not as they give it at home;
But whenever the wind blows down from the north I am hoping
    I shall acquire some wings: then I will fly away home.

from the Kalevala

The Pikebone Kantele

Steady old Väinämöinen
the everlasting singer
  prepares his fingers
  rubs his thumbs ready;
he sits on the rock of joy
on the song-boulder settles
  on the silver hill
  on the golden knoll;
he fingered the instrument
turned the curved thing on his knees
the kantele in his hands;
he uttered a word, spoke thus:
'Now, let him come and listen
who may not before have heard
the joy of eternal bards
the sound of the kantele!'

At that old Väinämöinen
began to play prettily
the sounding thing of pike-bones
the kantele of fishbones;
his fingers rose nimbly, his
  thumb lifted lightly:
  now joy waxed joyful
delight echoed like delight
music sounded like music
song had the effect of song;
  the pike's tooth tinkled
  the fish-tail poured forth
  the stallion's hairs called
the hairs of the steed rang out.
As old Väinämöinen played
there was none in the forest
  running on four legs
  or hopping on foot
that did not come to listen
marvel at the merriment:

the squirrels reached from leafy
   twig to leafy twig
   and the stoats turned up
   sat down on fences;
the elk skipped upon the heaths
and the lynxes made merry.
The wolf too woke on a swamp
and the bear rose on the heath
   from a den of pine
   from a spruce thicket;
the wolf ran long distances
the bear ranged over the heaths
sat down at last on a fence
and fling themselves at a gate:
the fence fell upon the rock
the gate toppled in the glade;
then they scrambled up a spruce
   they swung up a pine
to listen to the music
marvel at the merriment.

Tapiola's careful lord
Forestland's master himself
and all Tapio's people
   both lasses and lads
   climbed a mountain peak
to take note of the music;
the forest's mistress herself
Tapiola's careful wife
dresses up in blue stockings
   puts on red laces
squatted in a birch's crook
perched on an alder's warp, to
listen to the kantele
to take note of the music.

What birds of the air there were
   wheeling on two wings
   they too came whirling
   and speeding they sped
to listen to the delight
marvel at the merriment:

when the eagle at home heard
the fine music of Finland
it left its brood in the nest
    and took wing itself
to the sweet fellow's music
the strains of Väinämöinen;
from on high the eagle flew
    through the clouds the hawk
calloos from the deep billows
and swans from unfrozen swamps;
even little chaffinches
    and twittering birds
    buntings in hundreds
    nigh a thousand larks
    admired in the air
chattered upon his shoulders
as the father made merry
as Väinämöinen played on.

Yes, the air's nature-daughters
and the air's lovely lassies
marvelled at the merriment
listened to the kantele;
one on the sky's collar-bow
shimmered upon a rainbow
one on top of a small cloud
bloomed upon the russet edge.
That Moon-daughter, handsome lass,
the worthy maid Sun-daughter
    were holding their reeds
    raising their heddles
    weaving golden stuff
    and jingling silver
on the rim of the red cloud
upon the long rainbow's end;
    when they got to hear
the sound of that fine music
the reed slipped out of their grasp
the shuttle dropped from their hand
    the golden threads snapped
and the silver heddles clinked.

There was no creature
not in the water either
   moving with six fins
   the best shoal of fish
that did not come to listen
marvel at the merriment:
   the pike slink along
the water-dogs veer along
the salmon roamed from the crags
and the whitefish from the depths;
the little roach, the perch too
pollans and other fish too
drift side by side to the reeds
   wend their way shoreward
to listen to Väinö's tale
to take note of the music.

Ahto, king of the billows
the water's grass-bearded lord
draws himself to the surface
glides on a water lily;
there he listened to the joy
and he put this into words:
'I have not heard such before
   ever in this world
as Väinämöinen's music
as the eternal bard's joy!'
The scaup-daughter sisters, the
shore's reedy sisters-in-law
   were smoothing their hair
   brushing their tresses
with a brush of silver tip
   with a comb of gold;
they got to hear the strange sound
   and that fine music:
the comb slid in the water
the brush vanished in the wave
and the hair was left unsmoothed
   the locks half undone.
The water's mistress herself
the water's reed-breasted dame
now rises out of the sea

jerks herself out of the wave;
at the reedy edge she reared
she turns upward on a reef
   to hear that sound, the
music of Väinämöinen
for it was a wondrous sound
and the music very fine
and there she fell fast asleep
she sank down on her belly
on the back of a bright rock
the side of a thick boulder.

Then the old Väinämöinen
played for one day, played for two;
   there was no fellow
   nor any brave man
there was no man nor wife, nor
one who wore her hair in braids
who did not fall to weeping
   whose heart did not melt:
the young wept and the old wept
and the unmarried men wept
and the married fellows wept
   the half-grown boys wept
   both boys and maidens
and the little wenches too
for it was a wondrous sound
and the old man's music sweet.
Even from Väinämöinen
   a tear tumbled down:
the trickles dripped from his eyes
   the water-drops rolled
bigger round than cranberries
   and thicker than peas
   rounder than grouse eggs
and larger than swallows' heads.
The waters rolled from his eye
others oozed from the other
   dropped upon his cheeks
   upon his fair face
   down from his fair face
   upon his wide jaws

down from his wide jaws
upon his stout breast
down from his stout breast
to his sturdy knees
from his sturdy knees
upon his handsome insteps
down from his handsome insteps
to the ground beneath his feet
    through five woollen cloaks
    through his six gold belts
    seven blue waistcoats
    eight homespun caftans;
    the water-drops rolled
down from old Väinämöinen
to the shore of the blue sea
from the shore of the blue sea
down below the clear waters
    upon the black mud.

Then the old Väinämöinen
    put this into words:
'Is there among these youngsters –
    these youngsters so fair
    among this great kin
    these of grand background
one to gather up my tears
from below the clear waters?'

    The young there speak thus
    and the old answer:
'There's not among these youngsters –
    these youngsters so fair
    among this great kin
    these of grand background
one to gather up your tears
from below the clear waters.'

The old Väinämöinen said
    he uttered, spoke thus:
'Whoever brought back my tears
gathered up the water-drops
from below the clear waters
would get from me a coat of feathers.'

A raven came flapping up
and old Väinämöinen said:
   'Raven, fetch my tears
from below the clear waters
and I'll give you a coat of feathers.'
But the raven got nothing.

   A blue scaup heard that
   so the blue scaup came
and old Väinämöinen said:
   'Blue scaup, you often
   dive down with your beak
and cool off in the water
so go, gather up my tears
from below the clear waters!
You will get the best wages:
I will give you a coat of feathers.'

The scaup went to gather up
   Väinämöinen's tears
from below the clear waters
from the top of the black mud;
gathered the tears from the sea
carried them to Väinö's hand.
They had changed to other things
had grown to things that are fair:
into beads they had swollen
into pearls they had ripened
to be the delights of kings
and rulers' joys for ever.

from the Kanteletar

A Plank of Flesh

Whoever created me
whoever fashioned this wretch
   for this evil age
   with time running out
did not make me a word-smith
set me as a song-leader:
better it would be for me
   and better it were
to be a song-leader than
   a footstep-leader
   a causeway on swamp
a plank on dirty places.

   My great kin would, my
illustrious clan would wish me
to be a causeway on swamps
planks upon dirty places
somewhere to step on bad ground
a treestump on a well-path;
   they'd wish me to sink
in the swamp, fall on the rock
   be crushed in the dirt
   be jammed under roots.

   But don't, my great kin
my famous clan, don't wish me
to be a causeway on swamp
planks upon dirty places:
a plank of flesh will not hold
a bone log is slippery
will not let a poor man pass
or the ill-shod pound across.

Don't Propose on a Sunday

A mother advised her son
a parent the one she'd fledged
as anyone those she'd groomed
herself brought into the world.
Thus I heard my mother say
   the old woman speak:
'My offspring, my younger one
   my child, my baby
if you want to wed well, to
bring me a daughter-in-law
don't propose on a Sunday
on the church path don't betroth:
then even a piglet shines
and even a sow wears silk;
the very worst concubines
hurry along the church path
all got up in blue stockings
all made up in red laces
   their heads bound in silk
   their hair tied in braids.

'Weekdays are the better time:
do your wiving then, my boy!
Take one from the threshing-floor
from those holding flails choose one
from those grinding betroth one
who has her coat on crooked
or straight without meaning it
whose kerchief has hoarfrost on
her bottom dusty from the stamper
her body white from grinding!'

The Dance

The dance was not led by me
nor by my partner here: no,
the dance was brought from abroad
the caper led from yonder –
the White Sea of Archangel
the deep straits of Germany.
But no, not even from there –
    not a bit of it:
the dance was brought from further
the caper led from yonder –
from below green Viipuri
    the great Finnish town.
But no, not even from there –
    not a bit of it:
the dance was brought from further
the caper led from yonder –
from beyond Tallinn, beyond
the outskirts of Novgorod
across St Petersburg's yards
and through Viipuri the green.

The doors of Novgorod creaked
the portals of Narva mewed
the Finnish town's drawbridge dropped
the gates of Viipuri squealed
as the dance was led along
as the thing of joy was brought;
the horses drew it sweating
and the foals foamed as they trod,
water from the collar-bow
dripped, fat from the traces' tip
as the dance was led along
as the thing of joy was brought;
and the iron sledge clattered
the curly-birch strut thudded
the runner of birch rattled
the bird-cherry shaft-bow shook
as the dance was led along
as the thing of joy was brought;
    and grouse were moaning

on the sapling collar-bows
and squirrels were scurrying
along the shafts of maple
   black grouse were cooing
on the prow of the bright sleigh
as the dance was led along
as the thing of joy was brought;
the stumps leapt upon the heath
on the hill the pines pounded
the rocks upon the shore cracked
and the gravel moved about
as the dance was led along
as the thing of joy was brought;
the cows knocked over their pens
the oxen snapped their tethers
the women looked on smiling
the mistresses merrily
as the dance was led along
as the thing of joy was brought;
   and lords raised their hats
   and kings their helmets
   and old men their sticks
   and young boys their knees
as the dance was led along
as the thing of joy was brought.

The dance arrives in the yard
the joy under the windows:
   wait, I'll ask leave to
   lead the dance indoors.
   Whose leave shall I ask –
master's at the table head
the mistress's in the porch
the son's at the bench end, the
daughter's in the inglenook:
may I lead the dance indoors
the bird of joy to the floor?
The master uttered his word:
   'Lead your dance indoors
   lead your dancing-guest!
We shall kill the barren cow
for you all to pace the dance
and to play your game of joy.'

The dance slipped indoors, the joy
made its way into the room
stamping its feet on the steps
clapping its hands at the latch:
the stone oven moved about
the curly-birch post thudded
the floor of duck-bones rang out
and the golden roof echoed
    as the dance came in
        as the bird of joy stepped in.

Grinding Song

Mouth draws wolf into the trap
tongue draws stoat into the snare
will a maid into marriage
wish into another house.
    Grind, grind, young maiden
    grind, young maiden's will
    grind, hand and grind, foot
grind, mitten and grind, stocking
    grind, grindstone and grind
a maid to a husband's house:
she has a mind for a man
smoulders for the village boys.
A boat's will is for waters
    a ship's will for waves
a maid's will is for marriage
her wish for another house;
for a maid even at birth
    a daughter is lulled
from papa's to husband's house
from husband's house to Death's house.

Lullaby

Rock, rock my dark one
in a dark cradle –
a dark one rocking
in a dark cabin!

Rock the child to Tuonela
the child to the planks' embrace
    under turf to sleep
    underground to lie
for Death's children to sing to
for the grave's maidens to keep!

For Death's cradle is better
and the grave's cot is fairer
cleverer Death's dames, better
the grave's daughters-in-law, large
the cabin in Tuonela
and the grave has wide abodes.

St Stephen

Stephen is a stable-lad
in the ugly Herod's house;
he used to feed Herod's horse
    tend the stable-mount.
He took the horse to drink, the
covered gelding to the well
the blanket-back to the spring.
The spring splashed, the horse snorted
so Stephen the stable-lad
got down off the steed and looked
for something wrong on the ground
something wrong in the water;
saw nothing wrong on the ground
nothing wrong in the water.

'Why do you snort, raven's food
    and neigh, demons' horse?
There's nothing wrong on the ground
nothing wrong in the water.'
'For this I snort, raven's food
    and neigh, demons' horse:
there's a new star in the sky
there's a speck betwixt the clouds.'

And Stephen the stable-lad
    cast his eyes eastward
    looked to the north-west
looked all round the horizon:
he saw the star in the sky
saw the speck between the clouds.
    So, a fox ran up:
    'Poor fox, wretched boy!
    You are fleet of foot
    a lively mover:
    go now, take a look
round behind the copper slope
why the star is born to us
wherefore the new moon has gleamed!'
    The fox ran and sped
    ran a long way fast
    ranged afar swiftly
round behind the copper slope.

    It meets a herdsman
and the fox put this in words:
    'O my poor herdsman!
    Could you truly tell
why the star is born to us
the new star born in the sky?'
The herdsman put this in words:
'I both can and know how to:
why the star is born to us
the new star born in the sky
is because God has been born
the most merciful's appeared.'
    'Where has God been born
the most merciful appeared?'

'There God has been born
the most merciful's appeared –
there in little Bethlehem
the son of God has been born
in a horse's hay-outhouse
at a rough-hair's manger-end
   on the rushy sedge
   on the frozen dung.
There God has given birth, the
Creator's laid his offspring;
he'd not exchange his baby
for copper to be melted
   for gleaming silver
   for glittering gold
nor for the moon, for the sun
   for the good sunlight.'

The poor fox, the wretched boy
   now came back from there
from behind the copper slope
bringing the news as it came:
'Why the star's risen for us
the new star up in the sky
is because God's son is born
the most merciful's appeared.
The Creator has laid his
offspring upon horses' hay
   on the rushy sedge
   on the frozen dung;
he'd not exchange his baby
for copper to be melted
   for gleaming silver
   for glittering gold
nor for the moon, for the sun
   for the good sunlight.'

And Stephen the stable-lad
took the horse to the stable
   tossed hay before it
laid on the broadcloth blanket
   fitted on silk girths
and went to Herod's cabin

stopped in the doorway
stood at the end of the joists.
Ugly Herod in shirtsleeves
is eating, drinking, feasting
at the head of the table
with only his lawn shirt on;
Herod declared from his meal
snapped, leaning over his cup:
'Wash your hands, get at the food
   and feed Herod's horse!'

But Stephen the stable-lad
   put this into words:
   'Never in this age
not in a month of Sundays
shall I fodder Herod's horse
   tend Herodias' mount.
Let Herod feed it himself
   from this day forward
for a better birth is born
and a fairer power has grown.
   Now God has been born
the most merciful's appeared:
I've seen the star in the sky
seen the speck between the clouds.'

Herod declared from his meal
snapped, leaning over his cup:
   'You're telling the truth
   swearing without lies
only if this ox will low
and the blockhead will bellow
which is bones upon the floor
its flesh eaten, its bone gnawed
and its middle used as shoes
   all winter trod on.'

Well, the ox rose up to low
and the blockhead to bellow –
   rose to wag its tail
trample the earth with its feet
and Stephen the stable-lad
   put this into words:

'Now am I telling the truth
   swearing without lies?
   Now has God been born
the most merciful appeared?
For the ox rose up to low
and the blockhead to bellow.'

Herod declared from his meal
snapped, leaning over his cup:
   'You're telling the truth
   swearing without lies
only if this cock will crow
the son of a hen will screech
which lies roasted in the dish
   meat smeared with butter
   with its feathers fluffed
   with its limbs stiffened.'

Well, the cock rose up to crow
the son of a hen to screech
   to rattle its bones
   to fluff its feathers
and Stephen the stable-lad
   put this into words:
'Now am I telling the truth
   swearing without lies?
   Now has God been born
the most merciful appeared?
For the cock rose up to crow
the son of a hen to screech.'

Ugly Herod in shirtsleeves
flung a knife down on the floor
   and says with this word
   snaps this reprimand:
   'You're telling the truth
   swearing without lies
only if the knife will sprout
which I've slammed down on the boards
and which for one year was carved
for two carried in a sheath –
   if the knife-shaft sprouts
   and it puts out shoots.'

Well, the shaft began to sprout
the shoots to break into leaf
    and six shoots sprouted
with a sweet leaf on each one
and Stephen the stable-lad
    put this into words:
'Now am I telling the truth
    swearing without lies?
    Now has God been born
the most merciful appeared?
For the knife-shaft is sprouting
which you slammed down on the boards
    and the cock has crowed
which was roasting in the pan;
and what's more, the ox has lowed
which was bones upon the floor.
Now I am leaving Herod
and fleeing the pagan's host:
I take my faith from Jesus
my baptism from the Almighty.'

That made the great man angry:
    Herod turned ugly
and he waged a fiery war
upon the Almighty's neck
and a hundred men with swords
a thousand iron fellows
rose to kill the Creator
to bring down the Almighty.

On Rich and Poor

Old folk remember
and those today learn
how before their time
life was different here:
without the sun people lived
groped about without the moon
with candles sowing was done
planting performed with torches.
    At that time we lived
    without the sunshine
without the moonlight stumbled
with our fists fumbled the land
with our hands we sought out roads
with hands roads, with fingers swamps
    with candles we ploughed
    and furrowed with fire.

Who had covered up our sun
and who had hidden our moon?
Estonian witches covered the sun
German witches hid the moon!
We could not live without sun
nor manage without moonlight;
now, who would seek out the sun
    who spy out the moon?
    Who else if not God
    the one son of God?
    The one son of God
Turo the tough, crafty man
    promised he would go
    off to seek the moon
    to spy out the sun.
He wound up a ball of dreams
    took a jug of beer
    an ox horn of mead
thrust a whetstone in his breast
a brush in his shirt front, took
a stallion from the stable
    picked out the best foal
he mounted the black stallion

the horse with the flaxen mane
went off in search of the sun
in pursuit of the moonlight.

He set out along the road
   he rides, he reflects
he rode a mile down the road:
a log lies across the road
across and along the road
and he can't get past the log
he could not go over it
neither over nor under
nor could birds fly over it
nor could worms crawl under it.
Turo the tough, crafty man
took some beer out of the jug
some mead out of the ox horn
   splashed the beer on it
   and sprinkled his mead:
   the log split in two
an eternal road appeared
a track ancient as iron
   for the great, the small
   the middling to tread.

He went on a little way
he rode a mile down the road:
a hill lies across the road
across and along the road
and he can't get over it
cannot escape around it;
many men, many horses
are rotting under the hill.
Turo the tough, crafty man
took some beer out of the jug
some mead out of the ox horn
   spilled the mead on it
   and he splashed his beer:
   the hill fell in two
an eternal road was born
a track ancient as iron
   for the great, the small
   the middling to tread.

He rode on a little way
he did a mile down the road
and he comes upon a sea:
the sea lies across the road
and he can't get over it
cannot escape around it;
many men, many horses
cover the shore with their bones.
Turo the tough, crafty man
took some beer out of his jug
some mead out of the ox horn
   splashed the beer on it
   and sprinkled his mead;
but the sea would not heed that
so he said a word or two:
   the sea broke in two
an eternal road appeared
a track ancient as iron
   for the young, the old
   the middle-aged to stroll.

He rode on a little way
kept on down the road a bit
and the Demon's cabins loom
and the Demon's roofs glimmer;
there is one shed on a hill
and three maidens in the shed
   are scouring the moon
   and washing the sun.
Turo the tough, crafty man
   saw the moon gleaming
   and the sun shining
and he stepped to the shed door
   takes the ball of dreams
   lobbed the ball of dreams
   at the Demon's maids
and he got the maids to sleep.
   He shouldered the moon
put the sun upon his head
and sets off for his own lands
   for his homelands bound.

He rode on a little way
he did a mile down the road
and hears a rumbling behind
    so he glances back:
they are coming to catch him
    and to seize him fast.
Turo the tough, crafty man
took the whetstone from his breast
and tossed it from his shirt front
    before the pursuers:
    'Let a thick rock grow
    a thick, heavy rock
so they can't get over it
    over or round it!'

Turo the tough, crafty man
    rides forward from there
    made a day's journey
and a rumbling follows him
    so he glances back:
the Demon with his dread band
is again coming to catch
    and to seize him fast.
Turo the tough, crafty man
took the brush out of his breast
and tossed it from his shirt front
    before the pursuers:
    'Let a spruce wood grow
with iron boughs on the trees
    so they cannot go
    through it or past it!'
    There a spruce wood grew
with iron boughs on the trees
    and they cannot go
    through it or past it.

Turo the tough, crafty man
    came to his own lands
and brought the sun as he came
and with him conveyed the moon
and he put the sun to shine
the sunlight to make merry

in a gold-topped spruce
on the highest boughs
and the moon he raised to gleam
at the top of a tall pine:
the sun shone brightly
from the highest boughs
shone upon those with fathers
the rich, the happy
but not on the fatherless
the poor, the hapless.

Turo the tough, crafty man
took the sun from where it shone
from the highest boughs
to the lowest boughs:
the sun shone clearly
from the lowest boughs
shone upon the fatherless
the troubled, those full of care
but not on those with fathers
not on the lucky.

Turo the tough, crafty man
moved the sun from where it shone
from the lowest boughs to those
in the middle of the tree:
now the sun shone equally
on the rich and on the poor
shone upon those with fathers
the rich, the cherished
and upon the fatherless
the poor, the beggars;
and merrily the sun shone
sweetly the moon gleamed
on the doors of the lucky
on the thresholds of the poor.

KALLIO

The Glow-worm

Among the flowers a glow-worm
Was shining silently
Not knowing that its light was
Beheld above the lea.

A star was looking sweetly
Upon it from the height.
A snake came from its cranny
Ready to shed its spite.

It pitied the poor glow-worm
And without cause it spat.
'Without cause?' hissed the snake, 'but
Why did it shine like that?'

The Cricket

A cricket sang just for fun
    out of lusty joy
    blurted its delight
on a honey-sweet hummock
    beside mead-sweet flowers.

The sun shone. The turf's soft tips
the golden flowers on the lea
    were looking, listening
    as it chirped away.

'What do you sing, idle knave
what follies do you blurt out?
Get to work, for no belly
is filled by empty babble.

Rods for backs like yours!
Thus a certain ant
a most mean insect scolded
the cricket's innocent joy.

But it sang on just for fun
out of lusty joy
blurted its delight
on a   honey-sweet hummock
beside mead-sweet flowers.

JOHAN LUDVIG RUNEBERG

from Idylls and Epigrams

She came back from her sweetheart's tryst,
came with red hands. Her mother said:
Why are your hands so red, my girl?
I plucked some roses, said the girl,
and pricked my hands upon the thorns.
Again she came back from the tryst,
came with red lips. Her mother said:
Why are your lips so red, my girl?
I ate a raspberry, said the girl,
and now my lips are stained with juice.
Again she came back from the tryst,
came with pale cheeks. Her mother said:
Why are your cheeks so pale, my girl?
She said: O mother, dig a grave
and hide me there! Put up a cross
and on the cross carve as I say:
Once she came home, her hands were red,
made red between her lover's hands;
once she came home, her lips were red,
made red beneath her lover's lips;
then she came home, her cheeks were pale,
made pale by her lover's faithlessness.

*

Out on the Saarijärvi heaths
was Paul the yeoman's frosty farm
whose land he tilled with eager hands,
but from the Lord he awaited growth.
With wife and children there he dwelt,
ate his mean bread in sweat with them,
dug ditches, ploughed the land and sowed.
Spring came, drifts melted from the sedge
and then floods bore off half the shoots;
summer came, brought down showers of hail
that laid low half the ears of corn;
autumn came, frost took what was left.

And Paul's wife tore her hair and said:
Paul, Paul, unlucky man! Let's take
the staff: God has forsaken us.
To beg is hard, but to starve, worse.
Paul took his spouse's hand and said:
The Lord but tests, does not forsake.
Mix in the bread one half of bark
and twice more ditches I shall dig,
but from the Lord I'll await growth.
She put in the bread one half of bark
and twice more ditches her man dug,
he sold the sheep, bought rye and sowed.
Spring came, drifts melted from the sedge,
but then floods bore away no shoots;
summer came, brought down showers of hail
that laid low half the ears of corn;
autumn came, frost took what was left.
And Paul's wife smote her breast and said:
Paul, Paul, unlucky man! Let us
die, for God has forsaken us.
To die is hard, but to live, worse.
Paul took his spouse's hand and said:
The Lord but tests, does not forsake.
Mix in the bread twice as much bark,
twice bigger ditches I will dig,
but from the Lord I'll await growth.
She put in the bread twice as much bark,
twice bigger ditches her man dug,
he sold the cows, bought rye and sowed.
Spring came, drifts melted from the sedge,
but then floods bore away no shoots;
summer came, brought down showers of hail,
but they laid low no ear of corn;
autumn came, frost, far from the field,
let it wait golden to be reaped.
Then Paul fell on his knees and said:
The Lord but tests, does not forsake.
And then his wife knelt down and said:
The Lord but tests, does not forsake.
But joyfully she told her man:
Paul, take the sickle with delight:
now is the time to live glad days,

now is the time to cast off bark
and to bake bread from rye alone.
Paul took his spouse's hand and said:
O woman, this was but a test
not to forsake the next in need:
mix in the bread one half of bark
for frost has seized our neighbour's field.

The Girl's Seasons

A girl one winter morning
walked out in a frosty grove,
saw a withered rose and said:
Do not grieve, don't grieve, poor flower,
that your fairest time is gone!
You have loved, you've had your fun,
you've possessed your spring, your joy
before winter's cold reached you.
A worse fate befalls my heart,
spring and winter together:
a boy's eye is its spring day,
my mother's eye its winter.

The First Kiss

The evening star sat by a silver cloud,
from a dim grove a maiden asked aloud:
Say, evening star, what do they think in heaven
when to a sweetheart the first kiss is given?
And heaven's bashful daughter made reply:
The angel-host looks down out of the sky
and sees its bliss reflected in earth's deeps;
only Death turns his eyes away and weeps.

The One Moment

Alone I was,
he came alone,
beyond my way
his way was set.
He did not stay
but meant to stay,
he did not speak
but his look spoke. –
You strange to me,
well-known to me!
A day departs,
a year flies by,
one memory
pursues the next:
that brief moment
is ever mine,
that bitter, oh
that sweet moment.

from Legends

The Church

Hard times and bitter trials drove
Onni the yeoman from home, goods, wealth
deep into need and wretchedess;
then the years wrecked what fate had spared.
Seventy-five winters cloaked his head
in snow that no summer could melt.
One thing he had of all that once
had brought him joy, one thing – his trust
in the God who sent him boon and bane.
Now banished to the door he dwelt,
hidden, ignored, in another's home,
supported by the parish dole.

Midsummer Day dawned, and the folk
woke in the cabin; old and young
dressed in their Sunday clothes, and all
would haste to the temple of the Lord.
In the old man the same wish woke.
He went to the master and he said:
'Let me come with you to church today,
dear brother: all spring I have sat
full of woes in the inglenook,
nor heard God's word for half a year.'
The master pointed towards the lake:
a thick grey fog hung over it,
no shore, no wave, no island loomed.
'Will you yourself seek out the road,'
he said, 'no other boat will go;
but round the bay is far on foot
and there's no horse here now for you.'

When the old man heard the hard word
he slipped to the shore, untied the boat
and started rowing in the grey fog.
'Who leads the fish's path at sea,
the bird's path in the air, to come
where His law calls them, He shall guide
me too to find His church today.'

The moments passed, the old man saw
lake and mist only, lost his way,
his strength began to fail, the oar
felt heavier and the hand was numb.
When in the morning calm the bells
first rang across the bay and the sound
reached his ear, it was dull and faint,
and he was further from the church
than when first he had rowed away.
They rang a second time, a third,
and the sound came from further still.
The old man raised his eyes towards
the grey sky, as though questioning,
powerless, helpless, hopeless, lost.

But at that moment the boat slid
slowly and struck a rock: dimly
above it through the mist appeared
a shore, that bade the old man rest.
Ashore he stepped and looked around:
he knew the place, knew the lake isle
where young he'd landed so many times,
and on a bare rock he sat down
thoughtful, and darkness reigned, and gloom
filled his soul, earth and heaven too.

They rang together. – Was the old man
guarded by higher powers? – When now
hopeless he raised his eye to heaven
a bright blue streak parted the clouds,
a hint of light. In church the song
would have begun; on the lonely isle
the first breeze too among the leaves
was stirring now, and the first lark
was soaring skyward. Nature's sleep
had quickly vanished. Note on note
now followed, and new voices woke
in dale, on hill; a jubilee
rang through the fog, rang through the trees
round the old man who, seized by the joy
of song, forgot his griefs and woe
and joined in: that sweet summer hymn
'The time of flowers is coming' rang
tremulous, softly from his lips.

The time of flowers had come. No walls
had shut the summer of which he sang
away from him: its hotbeds grew
shoots at his feet, its singing birds
he heard and Christ whom he had named
lily of the valley, Sharon's flower,
came as a flower, a lily, warmed
his praying mind in every breeze.

When he had sung the hymn, the sky
had cleared, but in the lower air
a mist still lay. Then the sun rose

from the eastern clouds, flooded with light
the land and water under fog.
The air grew quiet, the winged flocks
sought rest, now every creature showed
a wish only to look, not sing;
the old man followed with his eye,
dumb with devotion, the light's way. –
The dim next minute was made clear.
Cape after cape emerged from fog,
island by island showed; a world
of beauty bloomed from the waste of shade,
took outlines, colours, light.
                              Long since
the morning hour had passed when, moved
and thankful, his gaze clear, his brow
unclouded, from his seat the old man
got up and went to the boat again.
But still he looked back in farewell
towards the shore. 'God's peace with you,'
so he was heard to say, 'all birds,
young brothers, sisters, people of God,
who with me today, in the same church,
have praised Him and His glory sung.
Thanks to you, heaven's interpreter,
bright sun, who now have preached to us,
inclined our hearts to know His goodness,
declared His works before our eycs.'

The Prayer

Once, when in pious, merry talk,
old Luther at his midday meal
as usual sat among close friends,
one of them spoke complaining thus:
'Hard, bad to live in is the world,
all tricky bustle, earthly care;
no wonder, then, so many sought
in cloister-calm a quiet they missed.
I too am tormented by the noise
of an untiring worldly strife.

Where I live, someone hammers, beats
without a break the whole day through;
however early I wake, the din
disturbs my morning act of faith.'

And Luther smiled and said: 'Disturbs?
Think rather: I have slept too long;
listen, my pious neighbour has
risen already for his prayer –
for prayer, my friend, is diligence
and work. So when the blacksmith wakes
and thinks: The Lord has given me
another day and strength to work,
and cheerfully begins to beat,
his weary panting is to our Lord
no less dear than your sighs, and his
hammer at heaven's gate will strike
perhaps more strongly than your prayers.'

from A Small Destiny

Since then I have asked no more

Why does spring so quickly pass,
why does summer not linger?
Thus I often used to think,
asked many, got no answer.

Since my beloved left me,
since to cold his warmth has turned,
all his summer turned winter,
since then I have asked no more,
only felt deep in my mind
that beauty must slip away,
that sweetness cannot linger.

from Tales of Ensign Stål

The Fifth Day of July

Now in the bright July sunshine
I feel so wonderfully fine
    this morning hour so clear;
come, young man, if our wills agree,
let's to the grove go, you and me,
    and gulp some summer air;
this day is for festivity.

When the old soldier had said so
he left his net, stood up to go
    and quietly took my hand;
then through the village off we went
across the meadow flower-besprent
    to the blue lake and strand,
in pearls clad by the dew's lament.

O what a heaven, what an earth!
From the old man no word came forth,
    he seemed only to look.
A tear at times down his cheek rained
until at last he pressed my hand
    and smiled and softly spoke:
Say, who could not die for this land?

I was silent. From my heart a glance
was my only answer, grasped at once;
    for nothing else he hoped.
And silence reigned a minute more;
he looked about him as before
    from the mound where we'd stopped.
Then he spoke up, his voice a roar:

Oh yes, young man, here from this strand
you see a little of that land
   which fatherland you call:
fair as here by the Virrat lakes
is Saimaa with its thousand rocks
   where Vuoksi's billows swell,
where Imatra in thunder breaks.

If you stood in the furthest north
you would see just as fine an earth
   below its fells so high;
and if you looked on its flat coast
washed by the Bothnian from the west,
   Finland before your eye
would kindle love within your breast.

But can you grasp now my idea
and understand the silent tear
   that makes my eye so glitter?
And this day, can you guess now why
it could become so sweet to me
   and for all that so bitter?
It is the fifth day of July.

A day dawns, fades into the dark;
how many leave at least a mark
   ere they are borne away?
The fifth day of July, I'll tell
the mark it left, I mind it well:
   seventeen years to the day
it is today since Duncker fell.

There was a people in Suomi-land,
there still is: led by sorrow's hand
   they take all in their stride,
they do not balk at sacrifice,
their courage quiet, their calm like ice,
   their faith has death defied –
that is the people we call us.

Today you see it in repose,
not destroyed, not attacked by foes,
    yet it stirs your heart's flame;
I saw it at its time of trial,
in frost, in hunger, strife and gale,
    I saw it then the same,
what do you think I felt the while?

I saw its blood flow day by day,
defeat I saw and victory,
    but no one quit the field;
where no sun rose to warm the troops
a warrior stood, a frozen corpse
    and still refused to yield,
though without home, though without hopes.

What patience was there, what manhood,
what strength in mind, what fire in blood,
    what calm whate'er befall,
what feats were not required of one
whom soon this people and these men
    their hero were to call
and worship still when he was gone?

But ask, if you should come across
a veteran, an old war-horse,
    one of that doughty band,
was there one man – enquire of him! –
who over all the prize would claim
    and loyally he'd respond:
Oh yes, sir, Duncker was his name.

From no high forebears did he come,
this man, but from a humble home
    in a place long forgot,
and won a greatness hardly dreamed,
became the land's pride, was acclaimed
    its strongest patriot,
and would, while Finland lives, be famed.

And now this glory's pure renown,
his love declared it for his own,
   the flame of his warm heart.
To his country he pledged his fate
as to a mother, to a mate –
   with all he'd gladly part:
this was the love that made him great.

He died; yet what a destiny
to die like him, allowed to be
   honoured before the grave;
oblivion's lake we would defy
and raise a green-clad isle on high
   out of its deepest wave;
that is to die, yet not to die.

Now beam, adorned with flowers, O land,
raise everywhere a leafy strand
   from waves that sun-warm lie
and let your fell-tops redly glow
and let your rivers shimmering flow
   and cast your Saimaa-eye
in splendour up at heaven's bow!

That memory, when on this day
it calls on Duncker's name, like me,
   to you may proudly turn
and say: Behold the glorious smile
this land wore as she took his all;
   say, can she make hearts burn?
For this bride did the hero fall.

JUHANA FREDRIK GRANLUND

Children's Song

Here below the North Star
Is our earthly home,
But beyond the stars lies
That to which we come.

Here like flowers we have but
Little time to go:
There life will be endless
As the angels know.

Here the heart is sighing,
Weeping fills the eye:
There all hearts are happy,
Eyes are full of joy.

There on wings of hope I
Send my little heart;
There is my true homeland,
There I will depart.

MIIHKALI PERTTUNEN

The Golden Bride

'Twas the smith Ilmollini
his head down, in bad spirits
   helmet all askew
went to the forge of the smiths
   took a little gold
a felt hatful of silver.

He set the young men blowing
   the hirelings pressing
but the serfs did not blow well
neither did the hirelings press.

He himself took to blowing:
he blew once, flapped the bellows
he blew twice, flapped the bellows
   now at the third time
a sword squeezed out of the fire
a gold-bladed from the heat.
The sword might be good-looking
but evil ways came of it:
every day it killed a man
even two on many days.

   He added more gold
a felt hatful of silver.
He set the old men blowing
but the old did not blow well
neither did the hirelings press.

He himself took to blowing:
he blew once, flapped the bellows
he blew twice, flapped the bellows
   now at the third time
a stallion squeezed from the fire
a golden-maned from the heat.
The stallion might have good looks
but evil ways came of it:
every day it killed a mare
even two on many days.

He added more gold
a felt hatful of silver
and he set the serfs blowing
and set the hirelings pressing
but the serfs did not blow well
neither did the hirelings press.

He himself took to blowing:
he blew once, flapped the bellows
he blew twice, flapped the bellows
   now at the third time
a maid squeezed out of the fire
a golden-locks from the heat.
The maid might be good-looking
but I do not know her ways.

And so during the first night
he kept himself in his cloak
he held tight in his fur coat:
that side certainly was warm
which was next to the wool cloak
   that side was freezing
which was next to the maid's side
icy as ice on the sea
   and as hard as rock.

So during the second night
he held tight in his fur coat
he kept himself in his cloak:
that side certainly was warm
which was next to the wool cloak
   that side was freezing
which was next to the maid's side.

And so during the third night
he kept himself in his cloak
he held tight in his fur coat:
that side certainly was warm
which was next to the wool cloak
   that side was freezing
which was next to the maid's side.

Let not those who come before
and let not those after them
make a maid's likeness in gold
finish her off in silver:
the breath of silver is chill
and the glow of gold is cold.

The Smith

By night born, Ilmollini
by day went to the smithy
    forged a hundred locks
    and a thousand keys.
No smith is better than he
and no craftsman more careful
though born on a charcoal hill
brought up on a coal-black heath.
    That smith is a god:
    he has forged the sky
beaten out the air's arches
and there is no hammer-mark
nor trace of where tongs have held
    of forked iron's rule.

ZACHRIS TOPELIUS

Christmas Song

Give me no gold, no rich reward
   at blessed Christmastide;
give me God's glory, angel-guard,
   let peace on earth abide!
     Give me a feast
     that gladdens best
the Master, my invited guest!
Give me no gold, no rich reward,
   give me an angel-guard!

Give me a home on native soil
   with children round the tree,
God's Word in lamplight after toil
   and darkness turned away!
     Give me a place,
     a state of grace,
glad trust and hope and faithfulness!
Give me a home on native soil
   and God's word after toil!

To high, to low, to rich, to poor
   come, holy Christmas peace,
child-glad, heart-warm, to mankind's door,
   that wintry strife may cease!
     You only whom
     no change can doom,
my Master and my King, O come
to high, to low, to rich, to poor,
   glad, heart-warm to our door!

Landscapes

Winter Evening

A forest road. Spruces, drifts, boulders, shadows.
To the left, traces of fire. Ravaged woodland,
half burnt, black treetrunks laid across the snow,
ghostly and weird, long arms stretched out in menace.
To the right, the moon, dangling in the spruce
and brightly highlighting a horse, a sleigh,
a man in furs. There is a merry trotting;
we think we hear a sleighbell's happy jingle:
before the sleigh a hound of noble stock
playfully sniffs the fresh tracks of a wolf.

Midsummer Night

So often painted, never reproduced!
No night, no day, no stars, no sun and moon,
and yet a landscape in transfigured light.
Southward the sky bright, northward a wall of cloud.
A hill, a plain, a river, a church tower,
a farm, a barn, a horse cropping the grass,
all lonely, simple, ordinary – why not?
What cannot be described, defeats the brush,
is the day's crown upon the brow of night.
All rests, is radiant. Whence comes the light?
Its spring bursts forth, but cannot be perceived.
It comes, not from the hills, not from the dales,
it shines on all. It is original,
in the air, on plain, on river, on what's built;
from objects it proceeds by itself, it is
the secret soul of each created thing
exhaling in the northern summer night
its hidden longing and its silent hope.
Go, master, you who choose where your lights are
and carefully dispose degrees of shade,
go, give us, if you can, the soul of nature,
night clear as day, a landscape without shadow!

JYRKI MALINEN

The Visit to Tuonela

Now, that old Väinämöini
set out for church, resplendent
above the other proud folk:
his springy sledge-runner split
his curly sledge-runner bumped
on the rocky road to church.

The old Väinämöini said:
'Is there one of the old folk
to go for spikes from Tuoni
a crowbar from Manala?'

And all the people answered:
'There is none of the old folk
to go for spikes from Tuoni
a crowbar from Manala.'

The old Väinämöini said:
'Is there one of the young folk
the rising generation
to go for spikes from Tuoni
the crowbar from Manala?'

And all the people answered:
'There is none of the young folk
to go for spikes from Tuoni
the crowbar from Manala.'

Then the old Väinämöini
went off for spikes from Tuoni
a crowbar from Manala.
Went to Tuonela's river:
there the daughters of Tuoni
iron-clawed, iron-fingered
spinners of an iron thread
were busy with their washing.

Then the old Väinämöini
  called out, shouted out:
'Bring a boat, girl of Tuoni
child of the grave, a vessel!'

The daughters of Tuoni said
the children of the grave clanked:
'When your business is stated
a boat will be brought to you.'

The old Väinämöini said:
'Iron brought me to Mana
and iron to Tuonela.'

The daughters of Tuoni said
the children of the grave clanked:
'If iron brought you to Mana
and iron to Tuonela
your garments would drip with gore
your clothes would be oozing blood.'

Then again he called out, shouted out:
'Bring a boat, girl of Tuoni
child of the grave, a vessel!'

The daughters of Tuoni said
the children of the grave clanked:
'When your business is stated
a boat will be brought to you.'

The old Väinämöini said:
'Fire has brought me to Mana
  fire to Tuonela.'

The daughters of Tuoni said
the children of the grave clanked:
'If fire brought you to Mana
  fire to Tuonela
your garments would be on fire
your clothes would be spitting sparks.'

Then the old Väinämöini
   called out, shouted out:
'Bring a boat, girl of Tuoni
child of the grave, a vessel!'

The daughters of Tuoni said
the children of the grave clanked:
'When your business is stated
a boat will be brought to you.'

The old Väinämöini said:
'I came for spikes from Tuoni
a crowbar from Manala.'

Then the daughters of Tuoni
iron-clawed, iron-fingered
spinners of an iron thread
   brought a little boat.
They treated the man as man
the hero like a hero:
they gave him food, gave him drink –
   some serpent-venom
   and some lizard-heads.
They even laid him to rest
   on a bed of silk
which was of serpent-venom.

Then the old Väinämöini
   felt his doom coming
his day of distress dawning:
changed himself to a brown worm
slithered into a lizard
swam across Tuoni's river.

Then he went to his people
himself put this into words:
   'Do not, young men, go
to Mana unless you're killed
to Tuonela unless dead.'

Then the old Väinämöini
drove off to church, resplendent
above the other proud folk.

A. OKSANEN

The Rapid-Shooter's Brides

Don't turn pale, darling Anna,
though the Switchback Rapid roars,
for it is never quiet
and is far beyond my powers;
but he who knows where its rocks are set
will find it meek and powerless yet.

So Will said to his Anna
and steps into his boat
and gave the boat its freedom
upon the rapid to float,
and to see how the Switchback is
William takes that bride of his.

How bright the moon this evening,
how glittery the stream!
No bird, no bough, no tree stirs,
only the stars don't dream:
how beautiful would death now be –
to die together, you and me!

So Anna murmured softly,
a tear rushes to her eye,
but then the rapid quickened
and forces the boat to fly;
but Will has learnt to ride its might
and doing so is his delight.

As a boy on this river
all the rapids he'd race
and many a time the Switchback
flung its spray in his face
and not a single rock could be found
he was not used to dodging round.

But in the rapid's tumult
just where its course ran straight,
there in her foaming mantle
the youngest nixie sate
watching over the river-god's flocks,
keeping an eye on the rapid's rocks.

A heart too has a nixie
though she is foam above,
and as on land, so in water
can flare the flame of love,
and upon Will this nixie has
long – alas, too long – fixed her gaze.

For now within her bosom
a strange desire has flamed;
her breast with sighs is ringing
but that cannot be named:
she takes her place amid the foam
and waits for William to come.

Will's boat comes rushing forward
like a tempest from the north:
now it is riding wave-crests,
now from a surge bursts forth.
Will in the stern fares fearless on,
but Anna's cheek is pale and wan.

With joyful heart the nixie
swims towards him apace:
That's Will! But who is with him?
It looks to me like a lass.
Alas for a nixie, 'tis all over:
my darling has a human lover!

The nixie resolves already
to avenge her shattered hope
and from the rapid's bottom
a rock she raises up:
against it William's boat is thrown
and he and his beloved drown.

Today in the Switchback Rapid
still stands the Nixie's Rock –
that rock whereon she ruined
Will's boat and all his luck;
but it is said that still she is tossed
in the water for the love she lost.

Finnish Sonnet

Old Väinämöinen could not have believed
that one among our singers now responds
to the great Sonnet, and within its bonds
sings what by heroes would be well received.

Our cuckoos sit upon no almond tree,
no Lauras meet us on the way to mass;
no wonder then if in the North's morass
the sonnet cannot echo Tuscany.

Yet how melodiously would it ring;
then to his burning hopes the Finn would bring
new fuel, a new source of energy

if by just putting on these singing-fetters
his language, reckoned cheap by would-be betters,
broke out of other bonds and then were free!

LARIN PARASKE

Advice to a Bride

Listen, maiden, while I sing
and listen while I tell you:
    bear ill will in mind
and beware of looks askance –
as you knew how to join us
know how to be one of us!

Work arrives in the morning
    and work means thinking:
    come indoors as three
with a sheet on your shoulder
a besom under your arm
you, wash the family's faces!
When you have finished your job
take the barley from the hearth
then hurry it to the quern
    sift the grains softly
carry them in on the lid
    and bake bread gently
    start it off nicely
so that no dry grains are left –
    only plain sourdough!

You have finished your job, then
    go to the tall stack:
    don't pick out firewood –
take even an aspen log
take even a stick of pine
    one of birch too snatch!
For if you pick out firewood
the hags will start gossiping
the village women will say
the women neighbours will say
the shrewd hags in the village
the sharp neighbourhood women
if you pick out firewood, they
will say, the village women:

'Where is this madwoman from –
Lapland, or wrung from Russia –
    to pick out firewood?'

When you have finished your job
    then you sweep the floor:
    don't sweep up children
    don't kick the piglets!
When there is bread in the house
    put bread in their hands;
when there's no bread in the house
put chips of wood in their hands:
a wood chip is a child's toy
it will keep a child amused.

For a Sprain

Jesus drove along the road
and Mary along the ground.
A tree trembled, the ground shook:
    Jesus' horse stumbled.
Jesus got down from the cart.
    Come here, Lord Jesus
    arrive here, good God
    to fit the sinews
    and to join the limbs:
join the flesh and fit the bones
put the limbs in their places
    put bone against bone
    and flesh against flesh
knot the sinews together
the small sinews end to end
the big sinews side by side!

Older

Sorrow brings songs to the mouth
   longing makes us weep
and draws water to the eyes.

I sang much when a child, I
shouted a lot when wilder
I banged my tongue when smaller:
I sang then of my childhood
and shouted of my folly.
Now I shout amid my cares
set forth in my bad spirits
set forth amid evil days.

I wept then without reason
without trouble I complained
when I wept on father's lap
and yelled under mother's arm
and kicked upon mother's knees:
now there's reason for poor me
now there is reason to weep
to complain of my troubles.

But who can I cry to now
and complain of my trouble?

Why I Have Come Here

This is why I have come here:
   to lay forth my games
   to perform my songs
   to tell forth my tales –
   not to sit about
not to prop up the doorpost
nor to stand beside the wall.

No joy for those who rejoice
no merriment for merrymakers:
joy's for those who sit about
merriment's for onlookers.

ALEKSIS KIVI

The Far Forest

Down from the hill the child came running,
     Down to his mother running,
Spoke, and his eyes were brightly shining:
     I have seen heaven's country.

'What are you saying, little darling,
     Of the far land of heaven?
Where did you see the blessed country?
     Tell me, my golden apple.'

Long on the mountain ridgeway standing,
     Casting my gaze north-eastward,
There I could see a bluish heath, a
     Forest of firs far distant.

Over the trees I saw a hillock,
     Fair where a lovely day shone,
And to the hillock's top a pathway
     Covered with golden sand ran.

When I saw this my heart began to
     Pine and my cheek was wetted,
Nor did I understand my tears, but
     I had seen heaven's country.

'Not so, my child; in blue skies yonder
     Heaven's uplifted hall is,
There shine the lamps, the golden crowns, and
     There is the seat where God sits.'

Not so, but there upon the skyline
     Where the far forest glimmers,
There is the world of happiness, and
     There is the blessed country.

The Bear Hunt

A brave troop of men skis forestward
   With guns and glittering spears,
On chains the ferocious dogs with them
   With eyes that blaze like a fire,
     When the first light
     From heaven's brow
   Casts off the gloom of the night
   And the sun lifts up its head.

Now northward the expedition moves
   And swishes over the snow,
Their hair full of frost on shoulders waves
   So fast it whistles along,
     And from ridge-ways
     A harsh wind blows
   And strikes the vales with its wings
   And the snowy forest stirs.

In Bruin's domain they stand at last
   Upon the height of the fell,
From there, if you glance towards the day,
   The world is gleaming below,
     And without beams
     The sun turns round
   To skirt the heaven and earth;
   And the distant woods are blue.

From chains the ferocious dogs are freed
   To go wherever they will,
Unspeaking the hunters go on skis
   Embattled in their desire,
     And Bruin, he
     Pricks up his ears
   And frosty spruces ring out
   With the voice of Spot and Dash.

The king of the backwoods, mossy-browed,
    Is startled out of his lair,
Though fire and though lead unload at him
    They cannot hinder his flight,
        But in the snow
        Purple the stains
    He leaves where thudding he trod
    To the shelter of the spruce.

The dogs give him chase, away he speeds
    And veers now this way, now that,
Towards him the men on skis make haste
    Across the wide-open ground;
        And as he pants
        In frantic flight
    And proudly holding his head
    He approaches, bloody hero.

But now comes a hunter's fiery lead
    And brings the hero to earth,
He rises again and headlong starts
    And gives a terrible roar;
        Now he is hit,
        And the snow whirls
    As Bruin, dogs and mankind
    On the fell-ridge come to grips.

At last the grim struggle is resolved
    By one man's glittering spear,
The beast in his bursting, burning breast
    Now feels the cold of the blade
        And he slumps down
        On his snow-bed
    And darker then is his gaze
    That before struck fire and flame.

Around the one crushed the hunters stand
    Rejoicing high on the fell;
From there, as you glance towards the day
    The world is gleaming below,
        And without beams
        The sun turns round
    To skirt the heaven and earth;
    And the distant woods grow dim.

They haste with their quarry home at last
   Through winter's brilliant night,
When wreathed in the sky the northern lights
   Are sparkling high on its brow,
     And the pale moon
     Still with a smile
   Is walking high in that glade
   As it tends the flock of stars.

First Communicants

A crowd of youngsters steps into the temple,
Young girls are stepping in dazzling white garments
     As bells ring out
   And the organ sighs its music;
   And a storm blows from the west.

A picture hangs on the wall by the altar:
The Son of Man glitters there on a cloud-bank
     Heroically,
   But his lips are smiling sweetly
   And his forehead brightly gleams.

Up there you see the green meadows of Sharon
Made blue by distance, and lofty the palm trees
     On Kidron's bank
   And the gloomy slopes of Hermon
   Underneath a glowing sky.

But now the festival music falls silent
And at the altar the guests are all standing;
     The preacher tells
   Of Gethsemane's deep twilight
   And of Zion's town nearby.

'With faith your shield, with the sword of the Spirit
Fight on, fight on and pursue consolation
     In heaven's meal,
   And a golden crown of honour
   You will gain in Zion's town.'

Once more the song and the music are swelling,
And low she bows, a young maiden so modest,
 At the altar's foot,
 And her bosom heaves and settles
 And her cheeks are flushing red.

A murmur booms in the dome of the temple,
It booms like pure golden rapids resounding
 On mountain walls
 And the Son of Man resplendent
 In the clouds on high you see.

The meal is over, and out of the temple
The youngsters step, and the girl through the tempest
 Walks full of sighs;
 And the Sirens' rippling forest
 Is a-flutter on her cheeks.

Song of My Heart

(from the novel *Seven Brothers*)

Grove of Death, grove of night's land!
There's a cradle of fine sand,
There I will bring my baby.

There 'tis merry for a child,
With Death's lord upon his field,
Tending the herd of Deathland.

There 'tis merry for a child,
When day closes to be lulled,
Folded by Deathland's maiden.

Merry for a darling child,
In a golden cradle sprawled,
Listening to the nightjar.

Thicket of Death, place of peace!
There pursuit and quarrel cease,
Far from the world's betrayals.

The Rajamäki Regiment
(from the novel *Seven Brothers*)

High up on Rajamäki
    A married couple live
Who carry on five businesses –
    On many trades they thrive.

Mick, the felt-hatted gaffer,
    Goes about gelding beasts
And often treads the boards besides
    As fiddler at feasts.

Another trade is lugging
    And flogging lumps of pitch;
He dowses too and shuts off blood –
    A regular white witch.

Kate, the snuff-sniffing gammer,
    Sucks at a cupping-horn
As in the sauna steam she toils
    Moving from crone to crone.

Five sons trail after them amid
    The perils of their course:
Harry, the eldest, jogs along
    Astride a hobby-horse;

The second son has bristly hair
    And Matthew he is called,
But Bumpkin is the nickname
    The rogue gets from the world;

After him comes a pair of twins,
    A sturdy brat each one,
While Mick has dubbed his youngest
    Tatterdemalion.

And that makes up our Regiment
    That sets out on a tramp;
The wagon now stands ready
    Upon the rubbish dump.

And they go grinding on their way
   Up hill, down dale, through ditch,
A-gelding and a-cupping
   And a-selling pitch.

Kate of the snuffy face prefers
   To take the shafts and lead,
While, pushing with a stick behind,
   Goes Mick chewing his quid.

Upon the cart are loaded
   Three brats, pitch in a sack,
A bag that's full of cupping-horns,
   Some oddments in a pack.

The urchins in the wagon
   With all their might protest,
But Kate shouts back and swears at them,
   And Mick shows them his fist.

In front of them goes Harry boy:
   See how he drives his nag!
Bumpkin brings up the rear: he has
   A bottle-cart to drag.

To a big village now they come:
   The gates are creaking – hark!
The yelling children run and hide,
   The dogs they whine and bark;

For many a pooch has cause to greet
   Mick with an eye gone wild
And Mick has threatened with his knife
   Many a curd-mouthed child.

That's why the house-dogs rave, that's why
   The children are afraid
When the Rajamäki Regiment
   Steps noisily inside.

Across the floor see Harry
   Upon his stallion dart,
And hear how Bumpkin rattles
   Bringing his bottle-cart!

But now a hefty kicking
    Comes from the maddened foal
And into bits flies Bumpkin's cart
    And the wretch starts to growl.

Kate grimly from the rubbish dump
    Fetches a fearsome lash
And gives that devil Harry
    A devil of a thrash.

But the twins at that moment
    Give her hair-net a twitch
And then their turn comes round to feel
    The sting of mother's switch.

Harry he wails and Bumpkin growls,
    The twins croak at the double,
And Kate she stamps her foot and shouts:
    'You trolls, you gipsy rabble!'

The din would drown out all the cranes
    On swamps so far away
And all the drunken horse-dealers
    Upon their market day.

But now the word is going round –
    Soon enough for the folks –
That Kate the Cupper has arrived
    And Hemmo's sauna smokes.

The sauna soon is full of crones –
    From all points they made tracks;
They swap the latest gossip
    With cupping-horns on their backs.

Kate's lips are smacking as she works,
    Her blade snicks through the skin,
Old Peg beneath Kate's fingernails
    Chats through a gap-toothed grin.

But what's the matter in the yard?
    Good Lord, what a commotion!
Sows, hogs are preaching, piglets
    Are hymning their devotion.

Why such a racket from the sows?
  Why are the shoats all screaming?
Look: at the entrance to the sty
  Mick's knife is ready, gleaming.

Now Mick has done his labours well
  And Kate has done the same;
Gaffer and gammer take their ease
  Together, with a dram.

Time to be off: towards the next
  Village they must be gone
And Mick, always a cheerful chap,
  Strikes up his signature tune.

Kate of the snuffy face prefers
  To take the shafts and lead,
While, pushing with a stick behind,
  Goes Mick, chewing his quid.

So there below a field just cleared
  They wend their motley way,
Seen off by all the village dogs
  Barking lustily.

The brats they whine and Kate she swears
  And Bumpkin growls and snarls,
Till Mick he pelts the dogs with stones
  And on the road sand whirls.

But finally the dreadful row
  Has gone on long enough:
The dogs turn homeward, now that they
  Have seen the strangers off.

Long enough too the children's tears
  Whose flood subsides at last,
For now the Rajamäki storm
  Has blown its worst and passed.

And yet once more the racket sounds
  Over at Ravenhill;
From the horizon you can hear
  The dwindling thunder roll.

Well, for the monstrous Regiment
   I have matched word with note
And now the moment has arrived
   To wet the songster's throat.

SUONIO

In Praise of Idleness

Others are full of praise for the diligent and their achievements –
    How they sweat at their toil, labouring, never at rest.
I sing: idleness is our best gift from the Creator
    Only as long as we know how to enjoy it aright.
Brother, be idle, and then your mortal frame will not weaken:
    Trouble and toil will betimes carry you down to the grave.
Be idle, for only thus will the great opportunities meet you:
    Diligence half way does, idleness everything can.
When you are troubled by ills, hard work may well aggravate them:
    Lie down quiet, in a trice you will be better again,
And if gnawing grief should dog you in all you are doing –
    Well, take a break, and soon slumber will reach you at last,
Slumber will reach you at last, will sow those grains of oblivion
    In your eyelids, and off you will be borne towards joy.
What are the arts? They are all of them works of the man who is idle:
    Beasts of burden are not favourite hosts of the Muse.
No? Then look at the saints in the almanac crowded together:
    See whether you can find one who was diligent there.
They were idle, the lot of them, idle they sprawled and they fattened:
    Who does nothing at all cannot be guilty of sin.
That's how the idle made it straight to the mansions of heaven:
    Since they made it themselves, others can make it as well.

PAAVO CAJANDER

The Queen Delivered

On a mountain peak there's a castle that overlooks a vale,
But wild as a grave and dismal, it makes the spirits fail:
Locked are its iron portals, no peep of light shows thence,
While ghostly guards in silence patrol the battlements.

Yet at times, when the night is quiet and light has fled the earth,
A tender gentle singing seems thence to issue forth:
A queen therein is singing, so talk in the valley goes,
But who she is, whence came she, there is not one who knows.

They say she was a lady who governed all the land,
Who was famous for her beauty over every sea and strand;
But once when day was dawning she vanished quite away,
And now the lord is pacing his hall both night and day.

At times when the guards are sleeping and quiet night arrives,
The hapless queen's fair bosom towards her freedom strives:
To the night she sings her song then, a song of grief and sorrow,
Of her beauty lost, her freedom, her visions of tomorrow.

One day there was a traveller who to the castle came,
And to the songs he listened and knew them all by name,
And now his breast is kindled, a strange fire burns within:
He goes back to his country and sings them to his kin.

And when again warm weather begins to blow ashore,
The bard, inspired now, touches his kantele once more,
And an unheard of music now flashes from his strings:
Of courage, fame and passion, of life's holiest he sings.

Who would not be enchanted, who'd not be moved to hear?
Who a sword would not be honing, not sharpening a spear?
But still within the castle the queen sings forth her grief:
Far yet is the deliverer, when will he bring relief?

Ah, he is coming coming! See there, he will get here soon:
The sun shines on his helmet, and on his sword the moon.
'Our mother shall be rescued' – so to his kin shouts he,
And his voice rings out like thunder: 'Who, who will follow me?'

Give up, she is gone for ever!' He only gathers speed.
'Your death is just behind you!' And still he does not heed,
But strides on up the mountain towards the castle then,
And when the champion storms it he is strong as a hundred men.

The iron portals crumble, the grave is yawning wide,
The band of guards is swaying like trees in tempest tried;
Now leaves and boughs are breaking, the very trunk now falls,
And as through tangled forest the hero's pathway calls.

'So you are free now, mother, deliverance is here;
The long dark night is over, come now where the sun shines clear!
Again your eyes will sparkle, again your cheeks will be red,
And woe betide whoever hurts one hair of your head!'

He leads out of the castle the queen into the light
And all the kin now hurry to greet them with delight,
And a tender, gentle singing seems once again to quiver,
But this is a song of morning, for the night is gone for ever.

The queen again is sitting enthroned in all her glory,
Her loveliness like the daylight, told everywhere her story.
On the mountain peak the castle is vanishing year by year;
Soon it will topple, and only a few scattered stones will appear.

In the Morning

Day has already arrived and the cheeks of nature are glowing
    As upon them the sun casts an affectionate look.
Even the grasses are rubbing sleep from their eyes and are lifting
    Off their mantle of mist, slowly they open their flowers.
Grouse whir up into flight and a duck quacks down in the rushes,
    Somewhere a tomtit chirps, preening its feathers as well.
Now in the heavens' sea of light may my soul go a-swimming
    Ere night's fogs once again cover it over with frost!
Vast as space may thoughts come crowding into my spirit
    Ere it is shackled again, locked in familiar chains!
But how dark my forebodings: joy and singing and youth are
    And evermore will remain kin of the morning, the sun.

Now let us sing, now let us rejoice, for lo, like a swan that
    Heads for the open sea, so does our hurrying craft;
Waves that splash as we go toss up their glittering silver,
    Heaven scatters its gold everywhere from above.
Wheresoever I look I behold this land of my fathers
    Clad in a garment of flowers, all decorated with pearls;
Shimmering there is a mountain and there is a cluster of islands
    Rearing out of their waves, crowned with a riot of flowers.

Birches gaze at themselves in lakes and – look for a moment! –
    One sunbeam has strayed into the gloom of the firs.
Meadows and fields I behold, and the hut where I for the first time
    Learnt of my country and saw some of its beautiful face.
Graves in rows I behold of heroes who, having brought their
    Mothers up to the church, yielded to death in their turn;
Corn on the graves now is rippling, the ears are nodding in fullness,
    Source of the blessings of life, here they abundantly flow.
Let it not be for us too, when the evening shadows are long, that
    Nothing but husk and chaff is to be reaped from our work!

Why am I worrying, though? For blue-eyed now is the morning:
    Morning and youth, these twain live in the fullness of hope.
Come then, my hope, rise up; O breast, your ideas are burning,
    Be like a sower and sow seeds of your land in the heart!
To the Creator's cellars fly as a bee and return with
    Honey for where you have sown, warmth to encourage your crops!
So that day when the bell summons you to repose from your labours
    It may be said that you did what you did for your land.

J.H. ERKKO

Christmas Eve

Is summer really coming
Amid the winter snow
And are the birds now nesting
For little ones to grow?

The spruce is sprouting candles
As though it were in flower
And doubtless it will lighten
The winter's darkest hour.

The old man now is youthful
And playing like a child,
His crooked back now straightens
And all things make him mild.

So kind and warm and tender
Is everybody's mood:
If only it were Christmas
Among all men for good!

Flowers at Pincio

Ah, you flowers of February,
   Flowers at Pincio!
   Could I but bear you
   To Finland, where you
To our northern land would bring
Some breath of eternal spring
And your eager scent would spill
From this ever verdant hill –
Ah, you flowers of February,
   Flowers at Pincio!

But, you delicate small flowers,
   Flowers at Pincio,
   You would not last
   The northern blast:
Only for your native bower
Were you born and will you flower.
For no grapevine ever strayed
To the northern lands and stayed,
Nor did flowers of February,
   Flowers at Pincio.

And yet if the spirit can
   Flower at Pincio,
   It need not die
   Where hard frosts lie:
Amid winter's frozen gloom
There a people learns to bloom,
There amid the ice and snow
Spirits can begin to grow,
To bear flowers in February
   As at Pincio.

Maiden, Sing

Little blue-eyed maiden,
Sit here on my knee,
Red-cheek, rose-mouth, choose it
For your singing-tree.

Sing to me, to others,
Sing to all the world,
That our hearts may not grow
Prematurely old.

Maiden, sing, that sorrow
May not crease the brow,
Nor grief break the spirit –
Hope sets days aglow.

Maiden, sing a bright sun
Over fields to rise,
Sing, encourage us for
Work, self-sacrifice.

Birds sing of their springtime,
Of their youth maids sing;
Finnish maids their heart's gold
To the whole world bring.

Bird of Grief

The starling, bird of grief,
Left in obscurity,
Had learned from life itself
Its little melody.

The starling, bird of gloom,
Sang but a little part,
But what it sang rang true
And touched the hearer's heart.

KAARLO KRAMSU

Ilkka

The deeds of Ilkka to this day
    the people's memory hallows:
he lived like any Finnish man
    and died upon the gallows.

Ilkka was but a peasant, he sprang
    from no great family,
but in his time the noblest son
    of Finland he came to be.

Into a storm of wild days he
    was flung by fortune's whim,
and yet he fitted in as though
    he had been made for them.

It was the grimmest time of all
    when tears flowed through the land
and the reins of our destiny
    were in Klaus Fleming's hand.

O many wept and sighed that law
    to ridicule was sent,
but while the others sighed and wept
    Ilkka did not lament.

No, when the folk elected him
    he gave them this advice:
'Endure your troubles if you must,
    but now you have a choice.

'The man who only moans and groans
    is prisoner of his woes:
he will get justice in the land
    only if he pursues.

'Struggling for freedom, let him keep
    this article of faith:
the path to happiness lies straight
    beside the shore of death!'

Into the air with greater speed
    no crossbow hurled its bolt:
these words flew out across the land
    and Finland rose in revolt.

Forthwith the flames of bloody war
    throughout the country spread,
and Finland never will forget
    the war that Ilkka made.

Though the oppressors met revenge
    in cruel hands, one day
treacherous plots struck Ilkka down
    at Nokia by Tampere.

While great works lead to glory, they
    can also shatter hope,
and Ilkka's straightest road they led
    straight to the end of a rope.

But these are Ilkka's words which still
    the people's memory hallows:
Better than living as a serf
    is death upon the gallows.

My Old Song

I sang a little song once,
it wasn't worth a lot,
but from my heart the song came
and told my inmost thought.

Some time passed – just a little.
The song came to my hand.
How odd! Why were there phrases
I didn't understand?

My song is out of date now,
its words have seen no change;
it is the heart that alters
and to itself grows strange.

ALPO NOPONEN

At Christmas Time

When snow has fallen and lakes are frozen
and when the eye of the sun is dim,
when forests silently lie deserted
by swallows flown to a distant clime,
a breath is warm in the winter weather
    at Christmas time!

Now none are thinking of care and sorrow
or feeling frost with its bitter bite,
a carol rings from the mouths of children
and eyes are glittering with delight,
the Christmas tree is ablaze with candles
    at Christmas time!

Good cheer our mother has spread before us
and now she gives and receives her gifts,
meanwhile the manger, the straw, the starlight
appear to eyes that belief uplifts –
and that's why Christians are tender-hearted
    at Christmas time!

VALTER JUVA

Spring in Karelia

Now trees are in leaf on Karelia's hills,
now every birchwood with foliage fills,
the cuckoo is calling and it is spring weather:
my helpless longing carries me thither.

I know your mountain ranges, your heights,
your smoky clearings, your dreaming nights,
your forests gloomy with ancient trees,
your glimmering bays, your estuaries.

There on my trackless way I would press
often through forest and wilderness,
and up a mountain bareheaded I bore me
where bold Karelia lay before me.

Or I went to the villages of men
in the high hills, a heroes' domain:
I saw honest labour done with good cheer
and I saw that Karelia's heart beats here.

Now trees are in leaf on Karelia's hills
now every birchwood with foliage fills,
the cuckoo is calling and it is spring weather:
my helpless longing carries me thither.

OTTO MANNINEN

Skating on the Sea

Unfrozen the dim inner waters below,
    but hidden in solid ice:
of the foaming billows underneath
    there is neither sound nor trace.

Unfrozen, the depths are rushing below,
    but on top is a level bridge:
whee! they can slip and slide about,
    leaving no groove or ridge.

Above, play is wild and laughter is loud,
    steel shoes all brightness and youth:
over the ice they merrily race,
    the lid on the gulfs is smooth.

Young life is on the loose and bored,
    freed from parental fuss:
so fair the forbidden path of desire –
    play can be serious.

Young life is on the loose and bored,
    the chest heaves, cheeks are aflame,
and the winds from the open sea bring dreams
    as they eagerly flock to the game.

It leads them to stretches blue with dusk
    where is no more buoy or mark:
no thought of black night surprising, no care
    about coming home in the dark,

nor any sense, already amid
    unknown expanses of sea,
of night descending to weave all round
    a moonlit mystery,

of having plumbed the inner depths
    to the point of drowning, where joy
with its capering burden already feels
    the floor giving way,

where the coolest composure is required
    to settle a foolish bet,
where laughing and leaping to one's feet
    no longer mends an upset,

where for the last time while still young
    one can turn with the dance,
where winter brings a week's work still
    and waters tempt mischance,

where, seeking the keenest ear, a tune
    of shattering beauty rings,
where, shot in the wing, a sea bird swims
    and a dying swan sings.

Embers

Firewood glow and ashes smoke,
grey becoming deeper grey;
a bright threat to bite the flame
redder in the middle way.

The brief rapture of a flash
brings a guest where your dreams dwell:
dreamy eyes are following
through the glow a fireside tale.

Silken lashes hood the eyes
dark, unsearchable beneath,
searching as the pictures change
in the fire strange books of death.

Embers glow and as they gaze
nightward shoot your best flare high.
Briefly you have lived a tale
of the sun and stars. Now die.

You Were My Joy

You were my joy, I was your woe;
I was night, your fire made my night glow.

Joys have fled but woes may stay:
things past, I know your vanity.

So thick shadows early pale;
the best memory wears a black veil.

Joys have fled but woes remain:
their pearls in your eyes secretly shine.

You glitter above more brilliantly,
stars of night. Winter is on the way.

Without Trace

Woe is me, ah, woe is me:
not one crumb of memory!
From men I was a moment gone
that I might not be alone.

While the friend was out of range
the talk of strangers sounded strange:
news of a death was given dry,
and the dead man, it was I.

I would not grieve or rush to blame
if memories remained the same,
if the fairest did not fade
and the best were not betrayed.

But the mind fills with distaste
when much goes and is not replaced:
joys and pains as blown sand flit,
and I built my house on it.

All things like the twilight waver,
which I thought would last for ever;
what I thought great withers later,
for the jaws of death are greater.

Memories die, are shut in earth:
the stranger, thought, looks, walks, back, forth.
Underfoot a loose stone knows:
someone has been and someone goes.

Musa Lapidaria

A wish for fantasy, wild games
    that never pause for rest,
a hand, a frail bewitching look,
    blood from the wave-god's breast.

On a blue road the morning's joy
    of flutes at glittering play,
above the hidden listening gulfs
    still onward and away!

Alas for the dreamer who believed
    in its jest of blue,
who came to play in the wave-god's shade,
    taking it for true.

So for treasure the billow thirsts
    buried in its blue pit,
and down it calls the stars, the suns
    bidding them dance with it,

and down it fetches, sparkling, young
    all the worlds of the heart:
amid the inner torches' delight
    the games bewitching dart.

But one into whom that yellow-curled
   Jack-o'-Lantern eats
has a sick heart that extinguished lies
   between his seaweed sheets.

A toy broken in play! The mood
   of the water-maid is dark:
widowed from play, her wish is then
   for the clamour of work.

In fire where no calm can be found
   even on its utmost shore,
from where even the hazy land
   can be seen nevermore,

the heart's defiance carves the rocks
   into the form of its dream
and the game like Jack-o'-Lantern in spring
   cannot make the blood stream.

It wants to shape in rock a myth
   that has no lasting abode,
that in blue bubbles foams away
   although it has drawn blood.

Diogenes

My footstep gains no ground from your great quarrels,
nor in your path do I intend to stand:
go, get your wreaths, enjoy them, never hand
victory to any, yours are the highest laurels.

With loads of gold – a back-breaking delight –
you, walls, arise; but where my lamp could measure,
the emptiest barrel seemed more full of treasure.
Upon that battlefield I will never fight.

Conquerors, wage your war, one such as no
immortal gods could ever win: for you
a healthy urge feeds drums and market day.

My envy is not roused by tradesmen's splendours:
when I was your age, fledgeling Alexanders,
I had dismissed whole worlds upon their way.

Still Waters

They nod at their reflection, these
irises, crowned with gold each head,
below them shifting, shining sands,
above them mayflies newly wed.

Below, the stream winks in the sun,
cool waters sliding in a dream,
above, a light of summer clouds,
the passage of day's golden team.

Above the clouds, beneath the waves
heaven's blue passing human scope,
lovely as that eternity
of peace for which the troubled hope.

As the stream's surface scintillates,
a fancy strays, a notion twists
sleepless, awake yet not awake,
and dances off to distant mists.

A dragonfly lets its blue wings
travel wherever it will turn,
a wisp of cloud sails far away
as shining bubbles water-borne...

O great, abundant summer peace
where calm and rippling waters lie,
you last, you linger – I know well –
but the bright twinkling of an eye.

The very next bend in the stream
might down a whirlpool gulp us whole
where the resplendent vault cannot
reflect the stream and so console.

Harmony, you who reconcile
great opposites to sweet repose,
sing like a stream to calm the foam
of bosoms haunted by their woes.

I know you will not keep intact,
your sheen a bright bubble, no more,
so glimmer in the soul's depths, gleam
while powers of light enjoy their hour.

Glisten with summer's blessing, lest
a notion gnaw us to be hence,
to pass down through the whirlpool's rage,
through the most final confluence.

So that, though fleeting in our breast,
your golden image may not fade,
as on the glittering wave-crest these
flowers shine, crowned with gold each head.

Jean Sibelius

Is only he a master who commands
millions with his yoke in many lands?
Is only he, whom clouds of incense bear,
great from the clattering armour he must wear?
Is he the richest, who piles gold yet higher? –
Why then should we acknowledge heaven's fire?
Hail to you, craftsman, master of sweet music!
The earth's oppressed will find in you their physic:
wherever with your melodies you call
no walls are narrow and no cabins small,
but arches soar, clear as the vault of sky
in festal glory, fervour, ecstasy,
a wing of sunlight flying far and wide,

the spirit's quest for beauty in full stride.
Hail to you, music's lord on Finnish soil!
The Nordic spell has yet to cease its toil
but still it rules despite the wealth of kings
and for the people's endless joy it rings.
The Vikings with their war-craft forged ahead,
they taxed, they ruled, they filled all folk with dread:
as music's craft speeds on beyond their sight,
the only tax demanded is delight;
your voyaging is many nations' pleasure
and your brief concord many ages' treasure.
In triumph you arrive, and castles quake
and bosoms yield to beauty in your wake.
None can resist the sceptre of your sounds;
your empire grows apace and knows no bounds.

Jardin d'Acclimatation

The wild beasts are behind bars, can't get out,
the tame are free to ramble, amble about;
your penny and the path from cage to cage
carry you round the world from edge to edge.
All from afar alive here you behold,
creatures of earth's primeval heat and cold:
temperate sorts you see, rapacious races,
at the same time you can put names to faces;
you see the airborne fliers, earthbound crawlers,
and creepers, climbers too in all their colours;
you see the monsters of the deep, the shark,
many of which must haunt you in the dark –
all creatures you can see gathered together,
screaming to fight, eat, mate with one another.
Here behind rods of steel they plant their paws
so silent, soft, you cannot see the claws;
their coats could be of silk, they are so smooth.
Do beasts lurk under them? Then face the truth.
You have an urge to stroke them, to draw near,
but there's an iron barrier, so stand clear!

What splendour, spring, what rhythm – as belong
to the most tuneful, touching, poetic song!
Restless they pace this way, that, then again:
a lifelong yearning fastened with a chain.
The blaze is dwindling in their fiery eyes...
What if...? Between you but a thin grid lies!
What if from there one of them suddenly
like Samson from his chains could burst away,
pushing you, crushing you! The thought of it
thrills, fills you now with dread, now with delight.
Jaws glisten and manes stiffen at a stranger
but they are isolated and no danger.
From Samson, Philistine, you turn elsewhere:
you are on pleasure bent, you do not care.
A shaggy head makes here no Nazirite:
your temple pillars will remain upright.
The tree of knowledge has spread wide for you:
you deserve sleep and food, diversion too.
You have seen all of nature in a smelter:
you have approached and yet remained in shelter.

No doubt you are still a child of a temperate zone,
seeking a pleasant Sunday afternoon.
You find this ready-made like thousands more:
months, years of gathering these was not your chore;
you see the work of ages in a bubble,
all but the paths of those who took the trouble –
so smooth the bridge across where you may go
from modern times to fossils of long ago.
You did not suffer dangerous unknown ways,
no cold, no hunger, thirst or sweltering days,
no desert heat, no freezing glacier,
no spikes or snakes to bite the traveller;
from the sea's troughs no tentacles could slink,
by night no vampires came to you to drink;
no ancient branch burst into leafy breath
or fell into the close embrace of death.
What others conquered, you may take in hand –
tribute from far-off water, sky and land;
yes, take in hand what lies within your powers,
but what you own is what's already yours.

From raiding motley nature's book you come:
have you too flown its heights, and its depths swum?
Out of the Labyrinth have you pushed your way?
Did you confront the Minotaur? Man, say!
Why did you strive to calm the monsters, or
did they win, show your strife its conqueror?
With them at large, do you now cowering hide
from something stronger yielding, pacified?
Was understanding granted or concealed?
Was your own hidden self in glass revealed?
And did some other world rise like a wall
from which an echo – albeit dumb – will call?
And will it, in a narrow circle curled,
lull you to thinking you've been round the world?
Although your fancy bears no trace of it,
in great and small its range is infinite,
and you may peer at every seismograph
only like curious moon-men, from far off.
Your own nerves are not tuned to understand
news of the rise or fall of some far land.

LARIN-KYÖSTI

The Liquid from the Tree of Life

Benaiah ben-Jehoiada stepped forward for a word:
'O Solomon, of Judah the king and mighty lord!' –
   a hundred men were under his command.

'The law of dust requires that you will soon be gone.
O do not die: without you Judah could not go on –
   you owe it to your people and your land!

'Behold, one of your servants has brought from Jordan's shore
this green dew from the eternal tree of life in flower,
   whereby man once from paradise was driven.

'Drink, lord, the holy liquid, and death you will not know,
for you will live for ever, and from us will not go:
   we'll gaze upon you like a light from heaven!'

'Benaiah ben-Jehoiada,' the king said with a sigh,
'just what is life eternal upon the earth if I
   live without love? It is a dried-out root!

'Were I alone, my night were a night of a thousand year:
what of my heart if never another heart were near,
   if my great kin should perish with its fruit?

'And if your friends should vanish, Benaiah, and you too,
none of you would return here, though I should call to you:
   only my voice would mock through empty rooms.

'What would Jerusalem then be, with its cypress flowers,
its cedars and its myrrh-scent, its herbs, its moonlit hours,
   unless my Shulamite were in my arms?

'I could not for her beauty shed bitter tears enough –
fairest of Judah's daughters and worthiest of my love,
   dancing among the vineyards of En-gedi.

'And how could I be gazing upon those fading eyes
when long ago their brightness my soul won for its prize
   to keep for dusk as well as for my heyday?

'On the roof of my palace I strolled when all was still,
expecting my beloved to tread Amana's hill:
  I'd never meet the lily of my dreams.

'Benaiah ben-Jehoiada, let this liquid wait
for the soil, to which in old age I'm promised as a mate:
  I'm finished, I'll go quiet when death comes.'

He spoke, and spilt the liquid, and down he smashed the cup,
and lo, a spruce tree sprouted, that straight away sprang up,
  and that is why the spruce is evergreen.

'And now at last, O Highest, *my* tree of life has died;
but love is all, and worthless is everything beside.
  Good night, Benaiah, now that you have seen!'

ARVID MÖRNE

The sea hurls a roller into the bay...

The sea hurls a roller into the bay.
The moonlit night's silver roller
whispers, glitters, ripples, shimmers
ceaselessly, for long hours the same.

Near the shore below black spruces
a man with a lantern treads a rocky path,
he is swathed in forest scent, silence, darkness,
– sees only the path,
the way home
lit by the lantern.

But in the forest
everything alive is alert,
quaking with fear
as a heel tip clinks against a flat stone.
The snake flees in terror and the grouse
quivers on its bough and the squirrel
scampers up the fir...hides in the top.

The man walks, stops, walks on.
Everything alive listens: a power is loose in the forest!
With one eye gleaming before him
a god treads the path with heavy step!

But from the sea, flooded in dazzling white moonlight,
a roller tumbles into the bay,
whispers, glimmers, hums
the lonely hum of the sea between dumb shores.

EINO LEINO

The Swing of the Gods

Whom the high gods take once upon their swing
they do not keep in one place
but throw about
between heaven and earth
until they bear away the light of reason.

And who is a crier of the might of worlds
today treads the edges of clouds
and tomorrow will lie
in the earth as deep
as a rapid that foams
in a mountain gorge.

Who swings on the swing of the gods
will not have long to live:
may that mortal see the peaks
of guilt, of innocence –
then may the dark night come.

Väinämöinen's Song

Not many joys are granted to mankind –
one delight in spring,
another in summer,
a third delight in autumn, high and clear;
to plough, to sow,
to gather together,
to rest in peace from labour at the last.

Not many griefs are granted to mankind –
one grief of the heart,
another from life's care
and a third grief at death, the high and stern;
a friend deceives us,
a life leaves us,
magic is only a hero's work and strength.

Why then should I, granted the kantele, sing
of other delights
and other sorrows?
I cannot read the stars on heaven's lid,
nor the fish in the sea,
nor the flowers in the grass;
so I sing what is granted to man to sing.

The brave man should not sing his arts, his parts,
not set them forth:
no, the hero
should sing about the changing years and weeks,
how the sparks kindle
and then die out,
and the workings of the law of death and life.

All else is but a gleam of heaven's arch,
fool's gold,
a splash of waves:
the hero ought to sing as the sea sings,
as one great great, holy,
one to be feared,
yet mild as night that settles on the earth.

So many songs, so many men of songs.
But there is one song
above the others –
the stern song of mankind, of thought, of nature.
Peoples fall,
but might will not,
sung by one whose might is his people's spirit.

from Whitsongs

Ylermi

Ylermi the proud master
drove in at the temple door,
spoke up from below the nave:
'Here is a man of the kind
who does not regret his deed,
who will not reform for gain.'

A boulder in the wall spoke,
a Virgin made of wood said:
'You will only regret it
when your house is in ashes.'

Ylermi the proud master
    rattled his shield then,
        charged across the heath;
he saw his house in ashes,
spoke up from the charred timbers:
'A new cabin will be built,
one more splendid than before.'

Ylermi the proud master
rode along the centre aisle,
    swore at the crossing:
'Here is a man of the kind
who does not kneel in ashes,
who is greater from his grief.'

A boulder in the wall spoke,
a stone Jesus uttered words:
'You'll only kneel in the ashes
    when your wife lies white.'

Ylermi the proud master
broke his whip of walrus bone,
    charged across the heath;
he saw his wife lying white,
    spoke up from the bench:

'Another wife will be got,
one more splendid than before.'

Ylermi the proud master
rode his horse to the altar
and blasphemed from the Lord's cloth:
'Here is a man of the kind
who does not grieve for what's gone,
like a storm he rushes on.'

A boulder in the wall spoke,
an icon called, bright-gilded:
'You will grieve for what is gone
only when your son is mad.'

Ylermi the proud master
stuck his spear into the floor,
    charged across the heath;
he saw that his son was mad,
from his belt seized his hatchet,
    and the father struck
his own son down to the ground.

He cried out vehemently:
'Another son will be had,
one more splendid than before.'

Ylermi the proud master
rode his horse through the window
among the people at mass;
the horse's muzzle blew fire
    and its eyes flashed white,
more those of the proud master
as he stood in the saddle.

'Here is a man of the kind
    who begs no pardon,
himself has loved with iron.'

A voice thundered from the clouds:
'You will only beg mercy
when you come to Tuoni's lands.'

Ylermi the proud master
  felt the floor give way,
  saw a flame leap up,
  drew his bloody sword,
flung his mitten on a stone
striking his hand off with it,
said even as he toppled:

'The church will fall down before
the mitten parts from the stone!
The walls will crumble before
the finger rots on the wall!
Before that, may a time come
too, another, harsher time
which will not bow down to death,
will not crawl off to Mana.'

He spurred the horse, and the flames
engulfed his golden helmet.
The mitten's on the stone still.

Saint George

  Saint George the high-born
  heard a girl screaming
beyond the fell of Turja;
  he rushed off to look.
  The heather-flowers moaned:
'The young maid was taken hence
in a sleigh with no reindeer,
in a sledge with no horned beast,
the collar-bow creaked, the road
whimpered, the girl wept and wailed.'

  Mist stood like a wall
beyond the fell of Turja
  and the worst frost stood
together with pitch darkness,
threatened to devour the man;
his gold-shod stallion snorted.

Saint George the high-born
with his sword struck at the mist,
   swished at the whiteness:
   'Through my holy love
brighten, eternal evening!'

And the swamp opened in front,
wet hummock and rotten pine,
the bottomless quagmires gushed
and the misty marsh-eyes looked,
threatened to swallow the man;
his silver-headed horse snorted.

   Saint George the high-born
struck the marsh with his bridle,
whacked it with his beaded belt:
   'Through my heart's sorrow
   harden, slack water!'

Iron rang out from the peat,
   from the marsh great swords
   and arms flexed rose up
under the eternal stars,
threatened to bring the man down;
his foaming stallion trembled.

   Saint George the high-born
   rose in his saddle,
said from under his visor:
   'Through the revealed God
I will rescue the young maid!'

   The man spurred his steed,
   rode upon axe-blades,
came to the shore of Ruija
where the icy billow rolled,
where the open sea was blue.

   The Ogress, choice dame,
lay upon a water-rock
in the Lapp sunshine; far off
her golden scales could be seen,

far away her bright hair glowed,
her blue crown was reflected
upon the foam-flecked boulder,
atop the eternal ice.

    The horse swerved aside,
    reared up on two legs.

    Saint George the high-born
taught his stallion with his whip,
    spoke up with this speech:
'Where's the girl taken from us,
    where the christened lass?'

    A blue lizard hissed:
'There are the fairest lasses,
the lovelier ones are ours,
    you must turn back now
    or your doom will come!'

In the water the Ogress
spat, the sea like rapids roared,
the breakers surged to the shore;
    Saint George the high-born
drove his horse into the waves,
    raised his gleaming sword
above the venom-dame's head:
'Tell me about the maiden,
you'll save your own wicked life.'

The snake-spiteful dame whimpered:
'There's the lass taken from you –
on the Water-demon's bed;
you seek a sorrowful girl,
you'll find a laughing woman.'

He turned pale in his saddle,
    Saint George the high-born:
    'Verily you've lied.'

    The evil-named mocked:
'Did you love the young maiden?'

He thought a moment, weary,
   Saint George the high-born,
he raised himself in his saddle,
spoke up in a steady voice:
'Yes, I loved the young woman
like a legend of heroes,
like an innocent hounded,
   like a fair one lost;
my holy star has fallen,
my bridegroom-love has risen.'

He struck the worm with his sword,
the lizard slid in the rock,
fire spurted from the blade's path,
   the stone flew in two;
under the rock a stairway,
a narrow, a dreadful lane.

He leapt off his horse's back,
   Saint George the high-born,
flung the reins on his stallion.
   'Take word to my land
if you hear that I am dead.'

The sorrowful horse whinnied:
'I will take word to the Lord
if I hear that you are dead.'

And he trod the rocky way,
   Saint George the high-born,
he found the laughing woman
on the Water-demon's bed;
and the hero's eyes darkened,
his voice rattled in his throat:
'Through the cross upon my breast,
   Lord, redeem your child!'

He killed the smiling woman
with his sword of fiery edge,
   Saint George the high-born,
the flower of all Christendom.

The Dark One

It was mamma's dark berry
   affrighted at birth,
he saw horrors everywhere
and beheld evil spirits,
   no good things at all.

His mother set him herding.
From the forest the herd-boy
returned, came home a stranger,
spoke with hair standing on end:
   'O mamma, do not
set me herding the cattle!
Lempo stood upon the marsh,
the demons neighed on the heath,
the devils ran after me,
the Earth-ghost rose from the earth.'

Herding was not for the boy.
   He was set fishing.

The boy returned from the sea,
   came home looking wan,
told with fingernails gone cold:
'Horrible the forest-folk,
the sea-folk more horrible!
   I saw Tursas come
   and the sea divide,
the Pale One sat on a rock,
   the Void gaped below.'

The sea was not for the boy.
He was set making a fire.

The boy returned from the fire,
   came home timidly,
   said with staring eyes:
'Frightful the sea's terrors are,
the fire's terrors more frightful!
The snakes spat sparks, the lizards
   spouted out red flame,
the Ogress cooked in the ash
and the Mean One turned the pot.'

The kin spoke of killing him:
'What work for the idle man!'

His mother hurried ahead,
drove him to the village games.

He returned from the village,
he did not dare to come home,
he kept starting in the lanes,
    hid behind the fields;
his mother found him standing
at the back of the farmyard.

The boy fell upon her neck:
'O my mother who bore me!
It is better that I flee,
better I go from these lands,
    go to Kalma's grove,
and flee to Tuonela's yards!
Grim things I have seen at home,
more ghastly in the village!
At the gate the Bare One stood,
the Bare One's son on the steps,
in the corner Mishap lurked,
the Bugbear loomed at the door.'

The mother knew her dark one,
she knew the doom-laden one
    was frightened at birth;
she wept, wept, did not reject,
she uttered, tenderly said:
    'You go, then, poor boy,
go to the spruces of death,
to the thicket of the dead,
behind the house papa built,
to the kind one's resting-place,
    where holy trees stand,
    where dim fir trees speak
    of those been, those gone,
in eternal night's sorrow.'

Papa woke in the tomb. 'Why
do you weep, pearl of the clan?'

'For this I weep, my father:
the forest does not like me.'

'Appease the grove with a song,
as your fathers did before.'

'For this I weep, my father:
the sea is no place for me.'

'Stay Ahti with offerings,
as your fathers did before.'

'For this I weep, my father:
fire is not a friend to me.'

   'Bind fire with irons,
as your fathers did before.'

Still the pearl of the clan wept.
'Why do you weep, O my joy?'

Pain burst into the open:
'O my father, take me too
with you to Kalma's mansions,
for I am mamma's dark child,
   affrighted at birth,
I see horrors everywhere,
but most in the life of men.'

From beneath the turf a voice
rose, a word strayed from Tuoni:
'Your fathers took fright before
and yet they lived out their time.
Desolate life's morning is,
death's evening more desolate.
Rooms are small in Tuonela,
underground chambers narrow,
no moon beams and no sun shines,
alone you'll sit, alone step,
the worm sifts the wall-timber,
you yourself will sift yourself
in perpetual regret
that is bitter, hard to bear.'

The boy returned from Tuoni,
    came, a quiet man,
sat in his beloved house;
he stirred the fire in the hearth,
busied himself with farm work
with smiling lips would murmur
    of forest spirits,
    of water spirits:
went to sea, to the forest,
took a net and set a trap,
and thus he lived all his life,
not rejoicing nor grieving,
piling up the days, as much
those coming as those passing,
the better much as the worse;
but the better ones on top.

Nocturne

The corncrake's song rings in my ears,
above the rye a full moon sails;
this summer night all sorrow clears
and woodsmoke drifts along the dales,
I do not laugh or grieve, or sigh;
the forest's darkness breathes nearby,
the red of clouds where day sinks deep,
the blue of windy hills asleep,
the twinflower's scent, the water's shade –
of these my heart's own song is made.

You, girl as sweet as summer hay,
my heart's great peace, I sing to you,
O my devotion, tune and play
a wreath of oak twigs, green and new.
I have stopped chasing Jack-o'-Lantern,
I hold gold from the Demon's mountain;
around me life tightens its ring,
time stops, the vane has ceased to swing;
the road before me through the gloom
is leading to the unknown room.

Elegy

Youth like a rolling stream is dwindling away,
life's golden reed beats threads already grey.
To no avail do I clasp the moment tight:
no merriment, no wine affords delight.

The proud days of my will are at an end,
what charmed my spirit is long since left behind.
I'm out of the trough. Must I go down again?
My only hope: an instant free from pain.

I know: peace will be granted me underground.
No sweet rest on the seeker's road is found,
the north wind blows, a storm blots out the sun,
red streaks the ice: don't mourn for beauty gone.

Sunk in the sea the flowering hills of my dream;
a poor man am I, with songs too dear to redeem.
I gave my all, my swinging-hour was brief;
I paid the gold of fantasy with grief.

I am exhausted, ah, to the very core!
Was it too great, the burden of rocks I bore?
Some would, but cannot: or am I one of those?
My gains are worthless, my results accuse.

Was every woe prolonged, was every chain
broken, was every dear boat burnt in vain?
Just as I need my all, am I sent reeling?
Do I freeze solid, just as my wounds are healing?

Hopeless a fight against the powers of heaven!
In song no solace is the singer given.
The frost calls, soon the broken tune will cease;
this beast slinks to its lair to die in peace.

Marjatta's Stars

The maid-mother's stars,
   the wide world's stars,
the stars of wise men as well,
   are glimmering slowly
   when night is holy
and the spirit of man is still;
they twinkle on cabins, on frostbitten farms
   and in great bridegrooms' hearts,
they rush into the muses' arms
   and a song on taut strings starts.

About that a tale
   to make men pale
the northern countries know:
   they are queer stars,
   the maid-mother's stars,
unlike our lamps below;
when her stars twinkle, they destroy
   or they work a heavenly change,
they threaten the boundlessness of joy
   or they overturn and avenge.

The night's wild hosts
   were spectres and ghosts;
a bride and her bridegroom walked.
   their twinkling dreams
   and the snow's wan gleams
in night's holy circle were locked;
the pines stood firm, devout and high,
   the moon showered miracles,
a light beyond the shores of the sky
   was stitching bridal veils.

Declared the bridegroom,
   the troubled bridegroom:
'Summer is on its way;
   we have love, which is
   our only riches,
but nowhere to sleep or stay.

To one who cannot be this world's slave
   the world will pay his due,
grant him some native soil for a grave;
   how sure of foot now are you?'

     Replied the woman,
     the earnest woman:
'This wintry way is our duty;
     though hardship will meet us,
     though gloom will beset us,
we bear a message of beauty.
We will walk carrying palms of love,
   truth sparkling overhead,
we will claim the light of the shores above:
   to courage I too was bred!'

     They twinkled, the stars,
     the maid–mother's stars
in their lofty constellations;
     forth stepped the ideas
     universal ideas
amid grim life's tribulations:
they cast a long beam whose brilliance spanned
   all the way from east to west,
they pressed the lovers hand to hand
   and bade them both make haste.

     The weeks they rolled past,
     the years they turned fast,
man kept the law of time;
     again summer wilted,
     again the snow melted,
but nobody heard from them.
On a strange shore their bones were blanched,
   in icy waters stirred;
to shield them beauty bloomed and branched,
   from them came not a word.

BERTEL GRIPENBERG

The Lattice Gate

You say the sonnet is but gaudy trim
that blends inanity with rhyme's carnivals
but shuts up life within its narrow walls
and puts the fire out on the hearth of dream.

A gold-wrought gate that has the wanderer foiled
the sonnet is, but over the wall a bough
weighed down with bloom hangs, by the gate comes through
a distant whisper from a distant world.

'This far, no further', the wind seems to purr.
Stop at the lattice gate, then, wanderer:
you have seen enough, no more is sought, you are free.

Before the gateway that will never creak
open, O hear the muffled singing quake
with greetings from the world you will never see.

A Lonely Ski Track

A lonely ski track finding
a way through forest deeps,
a lonely ski track winding
out over ridges and steeps,
over swamps where snow is driving
and pines squat few and short,
further and further striving:
that is the way of my thought.

A frozen ski track slipping
into forest quite alone,
a human life outstripping
others down paths unknown;

far off are answers resisting
questions the heart must bear:
across the snow-crust twisting
is my passage here and there.

A lonely ski track, ended
at a cliff's baffling edge
where windswept firs are suspended
on a sudden rocky ledge:
what are the bright stars calling?
How the forest fades to black,
how lightly the flakes are falling
upon the snowbound track!

JOEL LEHTONEN

from **Spring Symphony**

A country cousin's delight

Oh, my dear brother,
here we sit now in the pavilion
of the Korkeasaari zoo,
as the spring evening cools towards night.
A country cousin am I,
just visiting the capital
with May coming to an end.
Meeting now, we chums pass the evening
in talk, with tankards too.
No: dusk lightening the night.

We've been brought here
by a wind that grew weary, dropped in the sail
when the sun on Saturday
sank in the sea. With its domes
the fair city gleamed in silhouette;
only the top of the Uspensky church
still glowed red, glowed in the onions,
the earrings of Mother Russia
in her haughty, barbaric
blood-crimson.
Here now the groves are slumbering.
A craft waits, its slack sails
quivering like a butterfly's wings,
asleep. The bears in their lairs are snoring,
but in their high cages the Arctic
foxes are dashing about, and the stork
is dozing on one leg.

Aye, 'tis good
for us to be here, swathed
in blankets on the glass verandah
of Korkeasaari, my dear brother.
There below the window a flower-bed,
shading into night, gives off a smell.
Two candles before us

are bright. And what supreme
loveliness! What poetry there on the plates
when the splendid buffet has arrived,
borne by this handsome *buffetière*,
this noble Corinthian column!
A white, sweet-smelling cloth.
Bread, black and white –
rye bread with a lively taste
for those who've been working, like a big novel of ideas,
after that brisk sailing trip.
And white wheat, caraway bread
like a skilfully written romance
for someone weary of brain-work.
Sliced herrings, sardines,
quite as blind as ideas,
but virginal,
silvery, with soft scales they
swim in their thick oil.
Fennia vodka, clear as a spring!
Glasses, liquor: it glitters in the crystal
decanter as on Parnassus
the poem-spring in the temple's colonnade.
Small potatoes are steaming,
and ham, as rose-red as
the love of a young woman.
Pig's trotters, calves' foot jelly
trembling like a soul.
There are crunchy Russian gherkins!
A jellied pike is slumbering
pale beneath its gelatine cover
as long ago in her glass coffin
lay Snow-white, the fairy-tale princess.
There's salmon! There's burbot roe.
But the lobsters: like the mussels
they're prisoners of a narrow jar –
let's set them free!
Perhaps the shame of their imprisonment
makes them blush.
We're purple-fishers,
we hook them out as purple once
was fished off Tyre and Sidon.
And their delicious blood
presses our souls to crimson!

Splendid! we live by ideals!
Starting from the belly, as the belly
is often to blame for ideals,
the man whose belly asks for something
is at once a man of ideas.
There's goose liver, such that none
can name them all. With what more
does this hot food aim to delight us?
And punch has been ordered already,
to be brought by this *buffetière*,
who wears her hair in a crown
like the most stately Corinthian column.
A dram of spirit-bliss awaits us
after the physical life, the material world –
Palmroos's pale punch
with the green stopper.

So, my dear brother,
it's good for us to be here.
Those for whom it's not
can jump into Imatra's rapids.
Now, clear fennia, cheers!
And, my dear brother,
you, summoned to the capital
by the bore of work, a pleasant enough place
like this, from the Korkeasaari glass verandah! –
you who have wearily trudged
the street in showers, when spring here
is already drying up as in the Sahara,
and in the parks you may have greeted
every spring flower with a shout,
now you ask:
How have I been in the country?
What lingered over, what done?
How did this spring arrive at the edge
of a country you also love?
What was it like in the beautiful Homeland,
when did the ice melt
and the trees burst into bud!
Well, my dear brother,
I'm a country cousin in the mood for talk;
now to round off conversation I'll chat
about my Home Sweet Home.

L. ONERVA

In the Tropics

But once within a lifetime opens a fiery rose
that for but one night blossoms and in the morning goes;
out of its depths it fixes a hot inviting gaze
and in its glowing kernel are midnight ecstasies.

It has a leaf all bloody, it has a purple lip,
it has a dizzy fragrance like spring winds on the steppe.
Snap off the fiery flower and drink its nectar hot,
live and enjoy the moment, then drop dead on the spot!

V.A. KOSKENNIEMI

Sonnet About the Finnish Language

Like the dark murmurings of trees in the dawn wind
you are still morning-fresh in every part of you,
and like a waking fir on which a drop of dew
among its needles like a teardrop has remained.

Night slips into the maiden fancies of your vowels,
but from the sun your consonants draw energy.
Belief in triumph, highest gift of destiny,
has dressed them – look! – as it would warriors, in mails.

O Finnish language of my fathers, holy priestess
whose body, bashful, beautiful and wholly chaste is
still wrapped in pleats of lengthy adjectives unheard:

Petrarch, Dante, Shakespeare, the Muse herself are sleeping,
tucked away in your youthful bosom for safekeeping,
in the mysterious music of your every word.

from Elegies

You are alone, son of man, on your own in the middle of all things,
    you have been born on your own, you will depart on your own.
One step, another you think you are taking with someone beside you,
    now they are moving ahead, now they are trailing behind;
one moment, two you believe that the person pressing against you,
    man, is a kindred soul – it is a stranger you warmed!
Not one eye have you found that could meet your gaze and endure it,
    not one hand that did not slither away from your grasp.
Cold is the mood of a friend and cold is the breast of a lover:
    lips move, only the lips, nothing astir in the breast,
Someone will share your play, but not your delight or your pain:
    your most ardent desire dwindles away on its own.

Only your yearning has filled your void with a friend or a lover –
    phantoms that soon disappear once you have made an approach.
You are alone, then, man, on your own in the middle of all things,
    you have been born on your own, you will depart on your own,
hiding your errors alone and alone giving way to your heartbreak.
    None but your shadow will prove faithful to you, son of man.

Finlandia

(to Sibelius' tune)

Finland, behold, thy daylight now is dawning,
the threat of night has now been driven away.
The skylark calls across the light of morning,
the blue of heaven lets it have its way,
and now the day the powers of night is scorning:
thy daylight dawns, O Finland of ours!

Finland, arise, and raise towards the highest
thy head now crowned with mighty memory.
Finland, arise, for to the world thou criest
that thou hast thrown off thy slavery,
beneath oppression's yoke thou never liest.
Thy morning's come, O Finland of ours!

GUNNAR BJÖRLING

from Sun-Green

I don't write literature, I look for my face and fingers.
I came like the shadow of my trouble's joy,
I came like a longing for the great poem of life
and I carried my poem
like a day of life broken apart,
like a day of living that flowed in new forms, rich and made whole,
like a murmur of days brought together,
of the people I live with.

EDITH SÖDERGRAN

Day cools...

I

Day cools towards evening...
Drink the warmth from my hand,
my hand has the same blood as spring.
Take my hand, take my white arm,
take my narrow shoulders' longing...
It would be strange to feel,
for one night, a night like this,
your heavy head against my breast.

II

You cast your love's red rose
into my white embrace –
I clasp in my hot hands
your love's red rose that will soon fade...
O you cold-eyed master,
I accept the crown you offer me,
which bows my head down towards my heart...

III

I saw my lord for the first time today,
trembling I recognised him at once.
Already now I feel his heavy hand on my slight arm...
Where is my tinkling virgin laughter,
my womanly freedom with head held high?
Already now I feel his firm grip round my quivering body,
now I hear reality's harsh clank
against my frail frail dreams.

IV

You sought a flower
and found a fruit.
You sought a spring
and found a sea.
You sought a woman
and found a soul –
you are disappointed.

Vierge moderne

I am no woman. I am neuter.
I am a child, a page and a bold decision,
I am a laughing streak of scarlet sunlight...
I am a net to all greedy fish,
I am a toast to all women,
I am a step towards chance and ruin,
I am a leap into freedom and the self...
I am the blood's whisper in a man's ear,
I am a soul's ague, the flesh's longing and refusal,
I am an entry sign to a new paradise.
I am a flame, seeking and sprightly,
I am a water, deep but daring up to the knees,
I am fire and water in honest voluntary contact...

Pain

Happiness has no singers, happiness has no thoughts, happiness
          has nothing.
Beat your happiness till she breaks, for happiness is evil.
Happiness comes softly with morning's whisper in the sleeping thicket,
happiness slips away in light cloud-pictures over a deep blue deep,
happiness is the field that sleeps as noon glows
or the sea's endless stretch under blazing vertical beams,
happiness is powerless, she sleeps and breathes and knows of
          nothing...
Do you know pain? She is strong and great with secretly clenched
          fists.
Do you know pain? She is hopefully smiling with eyes that have
          wept.
Pain gives us everything we need –
she gives us the keys to the kingdom of death,
she pushes us in through the gate when still we waver.
Pain baptises children and watches with mothers
and forges all the golden wedding-rings.

Pain governs all, she smooths the thinker's brow,
she fixes the jewel round the desired woman's neck,
she stands at the door when the man comes out from his beloved...
What else does pain give her lovers?
I don't know any more.
She gives pearls and flowers, she gives songs and dreams,
she gives a thousand kisses that are all empty,
she gives the one kiss that is real.
She gives us our strange souls and weird fancies,
she gives us all the top prizes of life:
love, solitude and the face of death.

The Land that is not

I long for the land that is not,
for everything that is I am weary of craving.
The moon tells me in silver runes
about the land that is not.
The land where our every wish is wonderfully granted,
the land where all our chains fall off,
the land where we cool our torn brow
in the moon's dew.
My life was a hot illusion.
But one thing I have found and one thing I have really gained –
the road to the land that is not.

In the land that is not
my beloved walks with a sparkling crown.
Who is my beloved? The night is dark
and the stars tremble in reply.
Who is my beloved? What is his name?
The heavens arch higher and higher,
and a child of man drowns in endless mists
and knows no reply.
But a child of man is nothing but certainty.
And it stretches out its arms higher than all heavens.
And a reply comes: I am the one you love and always will love.

AARO HELLAAKOSKI

Conceptio Artis

Though thwarted, although thwarted,
with eyes firmly fixed I will
    press on like this,
    face forward still.

You got away. I had but
flounces, faded, far from new
    left in my fists
    from grabbing you,

but one day these paws will catch
you, put you in iron bands
    in spite of all
    your helpful friends.

Naked is how I want you,
unadorned and unpainted,
    by others' cheap
    gifts untainted.

I will show the world your form,
shout to any who hear me
    just as I saw
    you before me.

Dolce far niente

9 pm
the street's evening babble
cobblestones glow
like a colourful fable
your walk home under lamps in a row
    when   a merry hurry
       you return   a rumbling begins
           from work   the dull smile
                           of mannequins
     s h o p   w i n d o w s   g l e a m i n g
     t h o u s a n d s o f s t r a n g e r s t e e m i n g
        cars'
     feet
   paw
  the street
an eyeful
of light whirls at your head
    a white glove
           STOP
a white glove on an outstretched hand
      hrr–rr–rh
safely go man weary of day
your evening   your evening way   your way
windows glare wink peep
thoughts already sipping sleep
sweet sweet weariness
evening's passionate loveliness
           dolce far niente

ELMER DIKTONIUS

from The Jaguar

Sticking out of green leaves
red snout
eyes with
triangular glares
mottled;
whiskers wave-motion
claw-paws – why, you fly! jaguar of my heart –
how you fly and bite and tear and rip apart!
Your and my morality: to strike.

To bite is necessary while a bite gives life
to tear is holy while decay stinks
and life's ugliness must be ripped apart
till beauty and wholeness from its soil can grow.
That's how we are two, my poem and I, a claw.
One will we two are, a mouth a tooth.
Together we are one machine that strikes.

We will kill the yell of the unfeeling
the compassion of the heartless
the religiosity of the superstitious
the powerlessness of the strong
the evil weakness of the good;
we will give birth by killing
we will prepare a place
we will one day see
sunspots dancing.

Machine Song

(Orlodoffa doshkoff
orlodoffa doshkoff):
it's the machine –
me.

Rods and wheels
and
rivets screws and nuts
driving-belts (doshkoff) –
many men have made me
sledged and polished and hammered and filed
fine I'm fine (orlo)
shining
singing
ringing
shaking
floor and roof.
(No smoking!
Do not spit on the floor!
Smart dress only!
Do not drink from the carafe!
No admittance!
W.C. Office.)

Did you see the man who came yesterday?
He's crawling today on crutches,
and the girl who's humming today
will tomorrow be gutter-rubbish,
and the child they've produced
is like them and will be like them –
orlodoffa doshkoff –
my food.

(*Orlodoffa doshkoff*
orlo…orlo…orlo):
Oil and oil
(*ha…that's how I laugh!*)
human sweat and oil
and blood
(*he…that's how I roar!*).
The muscles shrink,
(*hi…that's how I grin!*)
skin turns yellow.
The neck is bowed
(*ho…that's how I sigh!*)
the kick up the backside
(*hu…that's how I hurry!*)
one more done for
(*away*).

Child in Starlight

There is a child
a newborn child
a rosy newborn child.

And the child is whimpering –
all children do.
And the mother puts the child to her breast:
then it falls quiet.
All human children do so.

And the roof is not quite tight –
not all roofs are.
And the star sticks
its silver snout through the gap,
seeking out the small one's head:
stars are fond of children.

And the mother looks up at the star
and understands –
all mothers understand.
And pressed the baby in fright
to her breast –
but the child sucks calmly in starlight:
all children suck in starlight.

It knows nothing yet about the cross:
no child knows.

TOIVO LYY

Genesis

That boundless, that beautiful Star!
It came from the unknown, afar.

Nor do I know where it was going,
but I know it set my heart glowing.

I saw it speed from beyond the dark,
glimmering at first, no more than a spark.

Myriads of centuries hurried its way.
Its loveliness shone ever growing on me.

Sowing lights on its track it beamed:
to me the proudest of stars it seemed!

To me no star could be more loved.
How I awaited my blest beloved!

It came, it came, ever nearer it drew!
Weaker and weaker my own strength grew.

More, more it tugged me into its field:
I had to yield!

I fell to a rending delight and woe:
I felt my powers go –

and I asked them to!
Towards its fire my fire I threw.

In each other for ever to drown!
A sun in the forge of a sun!

In my fiery hair I hid my virgin face
and towards my lover flung my embrace

and reached out my mouth – a
maid could do no other!

I sucked the glow madly with fiery lip.
I thought I would stifle in that hot grip.

I was blinded by joy and awe:
I only felt burning and heard a roar.

Nearer and nearer I sensed his charms:
a moment, and he would be in my arms!

He struck fire, a flame –
and my senses swam:

I was dead, mere chaos took over,
I felt every atom within me quiver!

Myriads of years thus went away whirling.
When I woke I sought the face of my darling,

but gone, gone was my lucky Star,
gone from me afar...

I saw it speed beyond the dark,
glimmering now, no more than a spark...

and it vanished out there.
Ah, where, where?

My heart with bitter longing shot through,
at first I noticed nothing new,

but soon across my path flashed clear
a little star, strangely near.

Never had there been such a one!
It followed another as I looked on...

Around me many had collected,
so tiny and so unprotected –

and suddenly my delight was enough:
they were children of my love!

They had been within my womb,
they were fire, from my fire come

and from me they had been hurled,
flame-clusters from my flame unfurled –

in them a fragment of my heart
and of my Star I saw depart!

Not quite departed, though gone afar,
that boundless, that beautiful Star!

P. MUSTAPÄÄ

Wintergarten

Hail, Ganymede! Now Zeus is dead, and yet
you with your eagle will live on for ever.
(A hurried side-glance at the programme sheet:
The Bermos, Catalani, Schöne Eva.)

...Or can it be, says Thompson to himself,
that England's policy is quite in vain...
It seems not to have worked in India,
they're half mad there, with murder on the brain...

...And I may not have mentioned it: this book
published in Denmark which I've lately had.
Then Mustapää has this to say out loud:
These Danish lyric poets are half mad...

...Well, Bonnelykke...Train-lyrics...But the evening
surrenders to the cello's funeral note:
The earth's so black, so black, so black the earth
and heaven so far away and so remote.

It has been granted as the lot of men
to live for one day, on the next to die.
...Oh. Night has come now to the Wintergarten,
now fades the glimmering landscape on the eye.

O Ganymede! Thompson and Mustapää,
two fellows here will keep alive your fable.
(Now they are leaving. All that then remains
is two drained tankards sitting on the table.)

KATRI VALA

The Earth

A fair angel of God
set out from his white heaven,
stopped on the delicate point of the moon's sickle
and from there looked on the Earth,
that glittering ball as it hurtled on its way.
Here fields bloomed and trees were green,
there fruits ripened and leaves turned yellow
and silent snowflakes covered the tracks of life.

And amid all that,
being born, growing, blossoming and dying
was man
who wept, laughed, hated and loved.
And there was more weeping than laughter
and more hatred than love.

But the Earth radiated a wondrous beauty.
From unseen flowers of the great virgin forests
a quivering fragrance rose
from whose midst the works of unnoticed love
ascended as everlasting royal lilies,
and weeping tinkled more beautifully than laughter.

And the angel yearned to leave his lofty spaces,
yearned to be a weeping, laughing, blooming, dying
speck of Earth's dust.

The Willow Whistle

I am no standard-bearer,
no eagle-hearted trail-blazer
on your journey to Jerusalem.
I am a willow by a stream
through which the winds blow,
from which the world's rebellious spirit
breaks off a simple whistle
to blow its tune
in which there is storm, pain, love
and a little of the new dawn.

RABBE ENCKELL

from **A Breath of Copper**

The sea works its memories
till they are ground smooth;
and still they mean so little.
For the sea itself is one
great memory
one great present.
So: demand of the phrase
the perfect leaf's velvet-soft gloss,
or force it to shape itself into a kneecap of rock!
How fortunate nothing is remembered,
nothing! And yet there was a testimony
about something past – a testimony in the bold
line of the face, in the freedom of the hand,
in the blankness of the mouth – a testimony in the voice.
And what you say is immaterial
as the crushed eggshells in an abandoned nest.

ARVI KIVIMAA

Arthur Honegger

Dashing along on the engine's buffers
no cap on her head
her hair flying free
heading for new lands:
Pacific!
Listen to the railway's thunderous music
listen to the engine shrilly whistling:
Here I come
– a   t r a i n
with sides gleaming black
haughty and beautiful
rushing and dashing
and with me is
Honegger
Honegger, Honegger!

SOLVEIG VON SCHOULTZ

A Way of Reckoning Time

A wingbeat flashed at the entrance to the cave
and the sun's parting was a bright green tuft
as we sank down and darkness swallowed us.
We crept through damp and narrow passages
where only the cold breathed, and suddenly
we stood upright in an enormous hall
whose roof soared dimly upward out of sight
whose echo bounded back from wall to wall
bewilderingly manifold, as if
voices from some forgotten time were kept
frozen within the acoustics of the cave.
The roof's thick fruit in heavy clusters hung
and over millions of years has dripped
its liquid chalk, a way of reckoning time.
We turned our torches on dark midnight blue
and red as of flayed bison carcasses.
Here folk lived sixty thousand years ago
the guide said, up there is an opening
into the next cave, man was agile then,
could climb, a hundred thousand years ago.
Then while the guide stood speaking we could see
another folk, the oldest folk of all.
They crouched together in their sopping cloaks
and bowed their necks low underneath the roof
where drops had dripped, dripped since time began
and where it had grown more with every drop.
A silent and long-suffering people, they
remembered most, hoarded their memories
and turned with dignity their backs on us
intruders, fleeting as this day and age.

AALE TYNNI

Not Mine...

Not mine to smite the rock,
to say: Let a spring break.
But I can find a spring,
can clear away the brush,
then sweep to let it rush
and put a cup to the brink
for the thirsty to drink.

What I can also do
is open a path through
thicket, and plant a rose
where the bright water flows.
And I can join days to days
and go my ways.

HELVI JUVONEN

The Boulder

I, a boulder
split off the mother rock
carried far by the ice
dumped by the ice,
am alone in the forest,
am odd.

I don't mind if children play
around me,
I don't mind if it snows
on my back. But
do not carve me
for I stand looking like a bear and think.
I am not cold. I too am warm
when the sun shines.

EILA KIVIKKAHO

In Folk Song Style

Timothy, by the ditch
you waving grass,
from you a girl and boy
one day would pass,
timothy,
you waving grass.

Watching
the foxtails
all those summer days
the village thought of a wedding
and this and that, but we knew
it was only summer days,
foxtails, warm-weather ways.

The harsh scythe mowed those days down,
took the hay,
and grateful was the one
that got away,
timothy,
you waving grass.

EEVA-LIISA MANNER

Bach

Is a stream,
rocks that form stepping-stones,
engraved dragons sleeping golden under water,
steps up to many white houses
worthy of Bruno's dust, of Pascal's polyphony of thought,
rest and freedom in a depth blue as Giotto.

Time suspended
builds a town
within which is another town,
bridges within which are other bridges
for snow-white horses and holy asses;
steps, echoes for conveying space, all of them perfect;

asses with haloes; sore nailed hoofs
drop off and bloom as the seven-petalled lily
you created
for angels to kiss –

asses with haloes, golden plates,
on each plate ten keys
like divine fingers
weaving music out of light and water

And gates are opening opening –
purple beaks open, are variation and flute,
flung wings open, lift, are a fugue,
towers ripple, locked towns shedding their doves
are a familiar mosaic, and here

Theorem

Let prose be hard, let it awake unrest.
But a poem is an echo that is heard when life is mute:

shadows sliding on mountains: an image of wind and clouds,
the movement of smoke or of life: bright, dim, bright,

a quietly flowing river, deep cloudy forests,
slowly decaying houses, lanes breathing warmth,

a threshold worn frail, the quiet of shadow,
a child's timid step into a room's dimness,

a letter from far away pushed under the door,
so big and white it fills the house,

or a day so stiff and bright you can hear
the sun nailing up the desolate blue door.

AILA MERILUOTO

Michal

God, how I despise.
With narrow lips, gleaming hair
I stand and despise.

And David, David dances.

Dances in a scant loincloth
with broad, bare chest, sweating,
on strong feet, clumsy
and his hair flying.
He dances a man's life:
too bare and too broad
with sweat-heavy days, strong nights...
He dances and does not see.

I see. Quite clearly I see.
Quite straight, quite tall I stay,
quite high I raise my head.
Of narrow build, tightly draped
with my mouth pressed tight,
my arms held hard at my sides
I merely stand there
and despise and see

when David, David dances.

He is like a big, wild land.
By turns he leaps up
with cliffs too steep, too rugged –
and with fertile fields
too wide, he calms himself.
And he is a land being formed,
he drives a peak forward,
an ever new, new plain,
but he does not stay to look,
not to know: this is.

Oh no – he wants more,
wants a strong land to advance
and rules it by his will,
but does not think: I rule.
He wants as if by dancing:
so, so he stamps his feet,
so with careless hands
he flings power into the void,
but he never feels, concludes:
Now I have been prodigal.

But I, Michal – I the tree,
the tree's shade, dark, noble
and quite clear – I see
how by watching myself
I see: every leaf stands out,
and I see: I see David,
and I see: I stand, despise
and despise and despise

and David, David dances.

HELENA ANHAVA

from **Dialogues**

The man goes forth in the morning to conquer the world,
promises to return at evening,
the woman remains at the window looking.

In the afternoon the children go forth.

The man returns, bent with age,
the woman by the window reflects:
The day seems to have gone,
I should have been busy with this and that.

'The children have gone already,' she says.
'You should have told them to wait,
now there's time to get acquainted.'
'Well, there's me, get acquainted with me.'

But the man does not answer,
is already asleep, a weary traveller.

BO CARPELAN

from The Courtyard

Mother spoke of her only a few times.
There was so little to say.
She had lived alone since her husband and only son
had drowned one July night off Högholm.
She greeted us silently and we greeted her silently back.
She was the only one to hang a Christmas wreath of cowberry
      twigs on her door.
The third Christmas it hung there late into January
and nothing was seen of her.
Mother was suspicious.
They found her, but I was not allowed to see.
Everything, mother told father, was neat and tidy
as if she had expected a caller.

from In Dark, in Light Rooms

It is not time that alters us,
it is space: the forest that was low as a dark ribbon
round the evening when we were children.
And the water that came up to our feet.

It is the road that is now straightened out,
the trees, the houses, the people the same
looking out of the windows
that are windows in space, not time.

Space, room for children, for lovers
where birds fly in and out,
spaces, rooms for one who sleeps so lightly
death's breathing cannot be heard.

It is the same furniture in the room,
the same branches in front
as if the room, the space were where you look
endlessly.

TUOMAS ANHAVA

from Poems 1961

Many and many the times when the trees have been blowing,
when the trees have been blowing, the air flying
below, above and past, many and many the times
I have been thinking
      and with wings puckering, like that,
and I have been thinking about flying,
in the act, flying like the air, blowing like the trees
and the wings, they
puckered up and I dropped
like the philosophers' stone, I dropped, in the act deeper
and still deeper I thought then
       about flying, like this:
with wings open (and tail), down at the front and up at the back,
          beat and beat
so simple it is, then
     I thought how
simple it is and deceptive, for
        if
flying requires wings, it is not complete, no,
not generally valid, no, not worth flying (and the tail:
where then will the tailless end up and how will the wingless
end up anywhere),
     and if
it requires air it is not flying at all,
nowhere near it,
     and if it requires
beats in the air
    it is
     worthless in the act
a diacatalectic spectacle
      between
      heights
      and
      depths,
thesis of wing to antithesis of air,
       synthesis, is that
flying
  I thought then and my thoughts

deepened and deepened, all the way to Germany,
and I grew weary and I sank into sleep, like that
with my eyes open, and wings opened,
                                    and the air,
in the twinkling of an eye the air rushed down, up and past me
and the ground (which is tailless) stretched up and flew,
the ground flew to where a magic carpet flies,
                                    and the trees, anticlockwise
the trees blew and the air flew, the sky's roof
came near as I went higher
and the clouds, which were raining below, shining above, looked,
they looked at all this without stirring, as in a storm
my eyes were open too, like this:
flying,
    flying in the act a metaphor,
an image in the air

LASSI NUMMI

from Chaconne

2

I've written many peculiar songs about peculiar things.
Today I'm going to write a serious song about a serious thing.
My subject is your ear. I've studied it, gone carefully into it,
observed it from all sides in streaming light, at dusk, in half-light
against a grapevine; while you're talking, laughing, and when you're
       silent;
when tea is brought in. During music, during a din, or when
       everything stops at once
and the distant rumble of the streets is borne on the night air
       through the open window.

3

Your ear – it's white but not like marble; I'd say that throughout
a warm reddish tint can be seen. The pretty labyrinth of grooves
       and ridges
– I'm using high-flown words on purpose – receives thus a deeper,
       more human meaning through solidarity
with living nature, transience and the splendour of moments.
       Towards it
various things gather, and its time is short; as a gleaming background
       it has the gold of your hair.

                        Towards it, past it
your hair gathers through a golden comb at the neck in a bun:
a swell glitters morning-fresh, through which, quite close to the
       shoreline,
a white labyrinth of clam or coral glimmers.

Towards it your features gather – these well-nigh unmoving and
       very lively features,
these Grecian, Asian features, unaware of their awareness, shut in
       their clarity – features of the Goddess of Grace, Mary, Diana,
these features of a birch reflected in a pool, of a maid, a girl, these
       white-stemmed features,
born from the smile of Artemis, from the smile fragmented in a
       spring, born to be Artemis,
born to be Diana.

Towards it voices gather – the roaring, whispering voices of the sea:
the sea-noise of the town, the noise of the garden's sea of leaves,
          which the giant clam of the house
repeats; the noise of the house, laughter and din and talk and
          murmur and music
and the call of a ship from afar; rustle of foliage, as though some
          brown god
were watching us without a sound.
                              Your ear's clam shell rests
on a seashore of voices. But the stillness has grown at its heart like
          a pearl.

PAAVO HAAVIKKO

from The Winter Palace

Fourth Poem

This poem intends to be a description,
and I want poetry that does not taste much,
    and I imagine
I am a thing that hopes like grass,

these lines are highly unlikely, for
this is a journey through a known language towards
    a region that is nowhere,
this poem is to be sung standing
    or read alone:

I also said that everything
    is outside and I am here,
I hung from trees like birds from trees
    and all the doors were locked open,
and I undersigned the passing day
    unread like a newspaper by the world,
its pointless sheet, and I sleep as a dream wakes,
    and in the dream I say: I.

This dense forest,
    few trees that are afraid,
and in this forest
    the voice is wet with sweat,

this is the region where trees unfold and within here
    a blind tree does not remember being seen,
hollow this place and everything so far, the forest
    unfolded flowers to my embarrassment,
and should I compare self with one unborn
    and doomed,
swallowed by flesh, pliant and soft
    and wholly female.

I did not now what it was like to be, somewhere,

I wanted to be silent,
I wanted to eat the words and change
perforce even as I was born.

This far I have come:
                              the house in the middle,
up to the table, towards the pen, as far as the paper,
here it is very northerly but my mind is dense,

and this is a poem I am writing in autumn, at night, alone
    and who is not me?
here everything is ordinary, here? here too:

someone who would like to be far off is delighted here in mid-autumn.

In this poem I am a mere image fully mind
    that does not ask why the fruit does not flower, and I wonder
who would care about this baggage of mine and this mind
    which I throw on the scale,
it floats in the air like a round ship, sluggish, sailing the wind,

I came through the forest and moved from line to line,

and the moment one is born one can peep at are there stars,
my unchecked greed is suddenly sad, the rain was pouring down
    and what is lyric poetry?
I want to tell:
a small house, narrow, tall and the room where I write this,
exaggeration!
                    but I imagine it all happening
and who is not alone and who is not a world?

I want to be silent about everything language is about.

I want to be back where I come from.

from Ten Poems from 1966

It is bad to begin, to write on the blank paper.
   And things bloom and wither,
                     it is almost routine,
but it does not help.
Of letters that now come one could almost keep just the envelopes
   giving one the chance to wonder sometimes
what was in them, and it is not that.
Thus many things are finally sealed up
   and if one were to open them, if someone did so
he would almost have to say that
   it is empty, there is no letter there.
But in matters of life and death almost everything
                      gets it wrong.

*

Let the sweet memory of you also fade, die, go away,
   for now that you have wholly settled into a dream
and dwell there,
   meeting there is pointless, painful, a parting.

*

The autumn chrysanthemums are somehow reminiscent
                   of a woman long in bloom.
Yellow, and many-coloured whose colours one remembers
   as one sees them.
To that extent they are like the fabrics of women's gowns.
Now white chrysanthemums come, and they bloom
   just as long as before.
But now they are alone in the room,
   no mirror, no fragrance, no woman.

from The One-and-Twenty

10

It happened on the night Crowson left jail,
  ran with a wing on the ground as a one-winged bird to the boat.

When it got crowded in the empress's anterooms
                Manforest the swordsman
                    made space,
  left the chambers, the night quarters of Zoe, the Hag of the North.
It was the second of the two years during which
  Byzantium in two years had four regimes,
                    crowded.
When it got crowded in the empress's anterooms
                Manforest the swordsman
                    made space,
  left the chambers, the night quarters of Zoe, the Hag of the North,
the nest of power, which power softens with feathers, its nest,
  the man left, mind and sword, for the boat,

they come, Broom, Whitefish, Big Toe and Fist,
                    Fishing and Pumpkin,
  the hundred and twenty claws and toes of the Sampo,
upon which it walks, on shoulders the Sampo, the *samppi*,
                the *sammi* itself,
  the Sampo covered in covers, concealed, stolen,
                    the 'bright-lid',
they bring it, it is brought to the wall, the precipice,
  a rope is tied to a pillar, the rope over a pulley,
so, straining the rope goes the hundred-and-twenty-toed Sampo.
  Whitefish, Big Toe and Fist, Fishing and Pumpkin
                bear off the hundred-toed two-stroke Sampo,
                    the soul of Byzantium:
its luck, its money's eternal worth that scorns the devaluer.

And it is lowered into the boat, where Manforest
                    brings the men from the Palace,
  those who watch, who watched the Gate, Orphan
                    brings to the place,
a count is made, and the count is complete, one-and-twenty.
  And each is the one, the others the twenty.
They leave Byzantium, like thieves in the night, robbers.

from Five Sequences About Life Rushing By

The soul is against the state,
   the willow against the jail.
No, it grows by the wall,
   a lifetime, with its roots,
outside the walls,
   a living shadow.
The soul is against the state,
   the willow against the jail.

from May, Eternal Month

I long to go far into the forest,
   away! into the streaming air.
When life has been lived, it
   does not taste much of anything.

So, life has been lived, in a house,
   in rooms, in a garden,
     through seasons.
At last! Autumn damp at evening.

   It makes the paper into a breathing
skin, makes the ink soakable.
   The paper breathes, now in.
The ink spreads, the paper stretches out.

JORMA ETTO

A Finn

A Finn is someone who answers when he is not asked,
asks when he is not answered, does not answer when he is asked,
someone who strays off the road, shouts on the shore
and on the opposite shore someone else like him shouts:
the forest rings, resounds, the pine trees sigh.
From there a Finn comes and groans, he is here and groans,
that way he goes and groans, he is like someone in the sauna and groans
when someone else throws water on the stones.
Such a Finn always has a chum,
he is never alone and the chum is a Finn.
Nothing can part a Finn from a Finn,
nothing except death and the police.

GÖSTA ÅGREN

R.S. Thomas

In vain he looks up
towards the deathly silent hunger
that is called space; patient-
ly he observes
spring's buds: they open,
sudden cries that stiffen
to bloom. It is a matter
of waiting. In November
he goes over to
the window. Yes, the landscape
shows again. Summer
was only its fleeting
body.

Lumberjacks 1950

They stand with dull fists
before the camera, helpless
in the huge jaw of
heaven and earth. Their
bodies are so spent
that one feels the same
queer shame as before
the dying man's eyes which
no longer manage to hide
him. These men themselves
never get a rest; they rest
their bodies, that part
of the soul which shows.
I scan the picture.
The eye-sockets' darkness
is plain, and the forest's
burden. But the hands are
waiting.

Gerd Ågren
(A backward child)

She looks at her body. There
is no soul that casts
this shadow. Her life
will never dwindle
to a higher meaning. Strong
as the heart that she is
she leads her pulse towards the
waiting wall's darkness.
Life is the only phase
in her life. She fondles
intensely; surrenders her
hands to your body. If life is
meaningless, it must be
a gift.

Europe's Cathedrals

They are the Middle Ages' huge
radio sets, tuned
to a station that without
a break broadcasts silence.
The message is that there is
a message; something so simple
words cannot declare. There is
a need for cathedrals. But
wave follows on wave; strength
grows to weariness. Like a
trackless heath the 13th century's
crowd of people stands under heaven.
Now our knowledge is greater,
but also our ignorance. The
stronger reality becomes,
the deeper is its shadow.

The pillars stand like longing
midriffs; hymns of light
stream in through the windows.
Night falls, the eyes
go out, the stars
burn.

Lyric Poetry

While spring aches
in the snow like a poem
in silence, and no one
sees the fire that roars
white where water
beats against rock, and
leaves, strong at last
from weariness, manage
to work loose, to sink
into the falls whose in-
visible pillars always
supported them, we speak
from this body,
constantly run through
by spears of blood from
the heart, protected only
by its existence, and all
we can say is
this.

To a Friend

To travel is
to reduce Samarkand
to reality. In the end
nothing else
remains. But also
the decision to stay
is a departure;
the crop yellows to fire
and knowledge becomes wordless
autumn. In the end only
Samarkand remains.

CLAES ANDERSSON

from **Poems from the Seabed**

There is a road no one has trodden
    before you.
Perhaps it is yours.
If you find it, it is yours.
It does not exist but does when
    you tread it.
When you look round it is gone.
How you got here no one knows, least
    of all yourself.

*

Whoever thought shadows lack colour
    has never lived with shadows.
Death's black shadows are blue, or dark blue.
There are light yellow shadows that escaped from
    childhood wallpaper.
When only the invisible was real, like
    the grown-ups behind the drapery in the hall.
As soon as papa disappeared it was blue, the
    colour when the shadows dance.
In our wood cellar there was a special kind of shadows
    you got splinters in your fingers from.
They are there still.
I live my life among the living and dead
    shadows.
The living shadows keep the dead shadows
    in the dance.
The dead love the dance of the living.
Because time has abandoned them, as the light leaves
    us when we stop dancing.

*

Like the beach we practise talking
    with our mouth full of stones.
A low rattle at sunset.

PENTTI SAARIKOSKI

from I Walk Where I Walk

In the market hall among the smell of meat and cheese and vegetables,
    in the Saturday afternoon rush when the little girl's
        balloon escaped, a red balloon
                rose quickly
            towards the blue roof structures,
        my works and days, quick trips
      when the sea has woken, the gulls are calling.
We are so powerless.
Upstairs in Nissen's café I looked at the pictures
      showing the old days when men
    used to sit round a table reading poems
        and smoking pipes,
  in Union Street the car roofs glinted in the sun,
      tulips and daffodils glittered.
I floated in the sea and watched the sun rise from behind
      green mountains, I thought nothing, felt I was
going with the world, moving, incompletely
    developing, I was alive, working, was
      a counter-system, oh to be
    back in Georgia,
          those days when my hands played
  merry games, the water splashed carefree!
I would sit, would wait
    for a poem to be finished in my head, then when it was,
      I would let it be forgotten, leave it there,
  chat with someone who would tell me
    about his life, his problems
      and his amorous conquests.
But surely we are glad when our child grows,
      we make plans
    that work out in time, we study places on maps
  where we want to travel, we sat once after sauna
    on the lakeshore as the sun went down
      and we felt
  envious of the underwater life of fish, pike, roach
    and perch, fine beasts.
The world, the form,
      the gulls call,
    when I love you, the backyard catches the morning light.

from The Dance Floor on the Mountain

On two tables I spread the old legends
the shields and the javelins and the fire-
spurting shoulders
man at war with man
the clank of armour
tumbling into the dust of the earth
and shrouded in the night of death
In the morning there was talk of war
of this one going on now
whose nature is bit by bit being revealed to us
this is not why men fall
or there is a shortage of soap
When we see what is happening to us
we know what they want of us
but we don't know who they are

When I walk to the seashore
the birds quit the tree
suddenly as if it were shedding its leaves
and I feel cold
I simplify the world into
a labyrinth
at whose heart the minotaur is panting
born of illicit love
an engine
whose motive power is living cells
whose job it is
to keep developing the labyrinth for its better protection

Only when the minotaur has been destroyed
and the labyrinth changed into a dance
is polity and politics possible again
This is the nature of the war going on now

It is not hard to find the minotaur
it is harder to destroy it
hardest of all to find the way out of the labyrinth

When I walk to the seashore, I intone
very clear, very clean

Aridela! Arihagne!
Underground cleanliness! Heavenly clarity!
So much faith is needed
that no one can
carry it alone
the old legends
on two tables,
I walk
to the seashore
each morning
to wait
so many years now that every sail
would look black in my eyes

from **Dances of Dusk**

a girl
pretty as a dandelion
took me by the hand and said
I am the light to lead you into the dark
There is no crop to boast of when I dig for potatoes
the summer was dry, I was lazy
pretty as a dandelion
We have to sleep jammed together
with legs curled up
these beds were not meant for people our size
I chatter with magpies about how all
the world's people
are my children and you are the light
pretty as a dandelion to lead
me into the dark
I have eaten the knowledge of good and evil, the sky is cloudy
philosophies and politics snap like dry branches

*

I am the way
                I walk along,
        a delegation, a theory, painfully
for I am an old man with authority
                                chosen for this task
        of going up the mountain, to a pedestal
                        from which I see the world's
                fields, the sea,
                people at their labours, a worker
        turning a concrete mixer, a farmer
                                watching over
                his tillage and in the post office
                        the mail being sorted and in the graveyard
the crosses rotting
                        I have come up the mountain to say goodbye
        to poetry, here they are, the carved statues
                        I no longer need to mention by name
they wrote books founded religions had themselves
                embalmed and they were embalmed
                        There were no blackberries this year at first
                                then some came
        small ones that finally when they got rain filled out
I sat on a rock, the rock I am sitting on
                        thinking
                This world is one big graveyard
                                one big goodbye and at last
I leave with no one saying goodbye
                        setting a cross on my grave to rot
                it is getting dark and the days
        are spacing out like evil-smelling railway carriages
                Freed from the sun's protection they
                                create art
                        that all the churches
                curse, I have seen
        can never forget that gesture

                        *

Dusk is dancing
there is no other world
than the one he
wrote with a skewer on a cow's skull
cobwebs hang from his fingers when he dances
he dances through the sentence he has written
You know nothing about this world unless you have looked
at a lizard eye to eye, this is how he dances
ants climb up his legs
piss
in his hairs, crawl
into his sperm-tube, eat away his
vigour, a snake
pushes its tongue deep into his ear and whispers
Not me
even if I know I will not tell
the water was high, the sea blackish
the waves growing higher from the shore outward
the wind bit into the neck, our business
our thoughts and wishes
remain facial expressions, it is difficult
to decide beforehand, to explain anything afterwards
I looked at the house on the mountain terrace, remembered the
war years
some late summer evening among cedars
when the grown-ups
were eating crayfish and toasting
I have never seen
I have never seen
any life in this house
though the road goes there sure enough
it is not a deserted house but unoccupied
I am too thin to fill my coat
The water is lapping over the stone steps
along the bottom fish are crawling on little feet
then night comes
night with long nails, holy darkness
to load the boat
I launch it
not knowing
where the sea will take it or who will unload the cargo

NOTES

p.21: *from* **Preface to the Psalter**. The final section of Agricola's preface to his translation (1551). The bishop – who is no poet – describes, in a confident past tense, the pagan gods of Häme, now a southern province of Finland but in his day a much wider area; then he turns to those of Karelia in the east where, thanks to the more lax attitude of Orthodoxy, some of them survived in oral epic down to the 19th century, and thence into the *Kalevala*. Tapio was the forest god, who lived in Tapiola ('Tapio's place'); Achti (Ahti), the water god, became an aspect of Lemminkäinen, but he also sails under his own colours in the *Kalevala* as Ahto. Äinemöinen (Väinämöinen) was a river god of sorts: Väinä is the Finnish name of the Western Dvina (Latvian Daugava) which enters the Baltic at Riga; but the god became a demiurge, assisting in the Creation, and finally a shaman, wise man, weaver of spells, the main character of the *Kalevala*. Ilmarinen (who also appears in this book as Ilmorinen and Ilmollini) was a sky god worshipped across north European Russia; in the *Kalevala* he is the smith who made the sky (see especially 'The Smith', p.127). Tontu (Tonttu) was a household god, now recruited in the plural as Father Christmas' helpers in red pointed caps. Wirankannos (Virokannas), the oat god in charge of fertility, came to be identified with St John the Baptist, whose feast falls at Midsummer: in the closing canto (50) of the *Kalevala* he fulfils his Christian role by baptising the virgin Marjatta's son. The Old Man (Ukko) is the supreme god who thunders: in modern Finnish, *ukkonen* ('little old man') means thunder. Hijsi (Hiisi) was a forest demon adopted by Christianity as Satan because he made a noise and disturbed study.

Agricola's preface, like much of his and his colleagues' work, is in a kind of *Knittelvers*, the rough rhymed verse of the German Mastersingers. Rhyme seems to confer respectability, as against the unrhymed, alliterative verse of oral tradition. He concludes his description of pagan beliefs with mockery:

> Eikö se Cansa wimmattu ole
> ioca neite wsko ia rucole.

> Are not a people's wits astray
> who trust in these and to them pray?

He goes on to tell how some benighted folk share commemorative meals with their dead. Well, the Tver' Karelians, descendants of religious refugees from Lutheranism who settled in the Tver' district near Moscow in the 17th century, still do it today, spreading tablecloths over their loved ones' graves and screeching laments that make one's hair stand on end.

p.23 A Ballad About St Henry... The oldest MS in the folklore archives of the Finnish Literature Society, this poem is thought to go back in oral tradition to the late 13th century. It seems to have been composed in oral style by a cleric to attract pilgrims to Henry's shrine near Turku. The poem recounts his martyrdom in 1156 by a murderer he had tried to bring to justice; the modern Finnish writer Veijo Meri has wrily observed that the latter – Lalli – is the earliest Finn whose name is known. Cf. *Kanteletar* 3:7.

'Cabbageland' renders *Kaalimaa* literally, a reading now preferred to an older reading of 'Wales, in England'.

p.26 *from* A Glad Song About Jesus: On Jesus' Descent into Hell. This foray into sacred epic (1690) has not only a title (*Ilo-Laulu Iesuxesta*) cast in the oral metre of its text, but also a summary in the same metre – and all on the title page:

> A GLAD SONG ABOUT JESUS:
> Solace from the Redeemer
> The Good News about his Birth
> Wondrous News about his Life
> Beautiful about his Death
> Joyful about his Rising
> Best about his Departure –
> All told in the Finnish Tongue
> For the benefit of Finns.

Much of the poem somewhat over-scrupulously sticks to versifying the Gospel; but in chapter 24, translated here, the muse has only the bald statement in the Apostles' Creed: 'He descended into hell.' For his account of the Harrowing of Hell the poet draws (like Langland 300 years before) on the apocryphal Gospel of Nicodemus with its images of a heroic Jesus battering down the infernal gates and shackling those within.

p.27 An Hymn... Finland's greatest Baroque poem – see foreword. Cajanus draws on a culture older than the Lutheran, which assumes Christian belief and does not need to evangelise. The poem's sombre tone is offset with flashes of typically Baroque imagination: most memorably, the silence of the stars becomes that of a remote God in the face of questioning man. The heavens declare the glory of God, says the Psalmist; but it is a cold glory. This poem deserves a place beside more celebrated explorations of the theme by Chassignet, Donne, Gryphius. Set to music by Uuno Klami (*Psalmus*, 1937).

p.31 From Oral Tradition. A selection of lyrics and charms; the greatest lyric bard, Larin Paraske, has her own place in this book (p.136).

Missing Him is one of 70 variants, collected from many parts of the Finnish-speaking area, of a lyric that made its first appearance in print in a travel book published (in French) in Stockholm in 1801; it was translated in 1810 by Goethe as *Finnisches Lied*. Cf. *Kanteletar* 2:43.

A Secret Bond: calloo is the more euphonious Scottish name for the longtailed duck (*Clangula hyemalis*), associated in Finnish tradition with sorrow. Cf. *Kanteletar* 2:124, 127.

Better Unborn. Cf. *Kanteletar* 1:46, *Kalevala* 4:217ff.

Grinding Song was the first Finnish oral poem to be printed. From 1766 the Turku scholar Henrik Gabriel Porthan published papers in Latin entitled *De Poësi Fennica*, which included this poem in 1778, the year of Herder's influential anthology *Stimmen der Völker in Liedern* ('Voices of the Nations in Songs'). The poem is what Finnish scholars call a 'chain' (*ketju*), consisting of several not necessarily related lyrics sung in succession. The grinding song proper runs only to the first 15 lines; the singer goes on to treat three other themes (including 'Missing Him' – see above), ending rather oddly with a sexual invitation. The text is remarkable in that it has not been 'corrected' or 'improved', as scholars in some parts of Europe were to do with their material: it is clearly a record of a performance, the central technique of what has come to be known as the Finnish Method. Cf. *Kanteletar* 2:209, 43, 53, 50.

The Muster is from the tradition of lyrics and laments which developed especially in Ingria to mourn the departure of young men conscripted into the Russian army. The tradition uses heroic elements in an unheroic way to express the feelings of women who would probably never see the conscripts again.

Epilogue. One of many used to end a performance; there are many prologues too. 'Cuckoo-caller' renders the nonce word *kukkuja*, literally 'cuckoo-er', i.e. singer.

p.38 A Lament for Booze... A peasant poem in oral style, printed in response to a law passed in the reign of the Swedish king Gustav III banning the home manufacture of spirit alcohol. The lines beginning 'If you, one I know, came now' parody the 'Missing Him' theme.

p.40 The Death of Elina (first-syllable stress, as always in Finnish). The outstanding work of oral tradition to survive in western Finland, this poem travelled widely, to judge from fragments of it collected in Ingria. The variant translated here was clearly intended for dramatic performance. A terrible tale of jealousy and murder, it recounts events at the manor of Laukko (still there) near Tampere in the 15th century. The villain of the piece, Klavus Kurki, merges two men – Klaus Kurki, lord of Laukko 1450-70, a district judge who tried to stamp out witchcraft (cf. the reference to 'Pohja wizards'), and Klaus Djäkn, another district judge, who burnt his wife to death and married a woman called Kristina (Kirsti) at least 50 years before.

p.47 The Sampo. The great trophy of Finnish myth has never been identified: generations of scholars have guessed, but their modern successors, content that the bards themselves did not know what it was, have stopped guessing. In the *Kalevala* it is a magic mill that confers wealth on its owner. Arhippa Perttunen of Archangel Karelia (some 600 km north of St Petersburg) was the greatest of the male bards, and this 402-line performance to Lönnrot (compiler of the *Kalevala*) in 1834 is reckoned one of the greatest works of Finnish oral tradition.

Oral poetry is built on formulas – set epithets, set turns of phrase, set lines – which a bard manipulated according to his (or her) skill. This formulaic construction is especially noticeable in oral epic, where it is an important memory aid: the description of it in Serbian oral epic by the American scholars Parry and Lord earlier this century revolutionised

Homeric studies. The present text abounds in such formulas. Our reading of Finnish oral epic is inevitably conditioned by the *Kalevala*, which imposes a continuous narrative on hundreds of largely disconnected fragments. For example, what are we to make of the opening formula 'The Laplander, the slit-eyed' and of what follows? The bard's listeners knew he was a young rival of Väinämöinen. The *Kalevala* fills out its own picture: he is Joukahainen, brother of Väinämöinen's chosen Aino, who drowns herself to avoid marrying him… Even so, the *Kalevala* may provide an approach to the present text, which can be divided into three episodes:

1. Väinämöinen, defeated, finds himself in Pohjola, the North Land, sometimes identified with Lapland but quite unconnected with 'the Laplander' (cf. cantos 6-7).
2. 'The gap-toothed crone', mistress of the North Land, agrees to arrange Väinämöinen's return home in exchange for the making of the Sampo by the smith Ilmorinen (Ilmarinen; cf. canto 10).
3. Väinämöinen decides that the Sampo, being so successful, must be stolen, which it is, to no one's advantage (cf. cantos 42-43). In the Kalevala this episode is considerably separated from its predecessors, to suggest the passage of time; we are also told that Väinämöinen and his people in the south have fallen on hard times.

p.57 The Messiah. One of the greatest expressions in Finnish of 'barbarian' Christianity, which combines Christian and pagan elements in ways that would surprise those nearer to the mainstream of Christian doctrine. Cf. early Celtic Christianity, which hailed Virgil, on the strength of his 4th Eclogue, not only as a prophet – he is Dante's guide in the *Commedia* – but as a magician, in which role he survives in the modern Welsh word for chemist, *fferyllydd*; and the 'Thomas Christians' of south India, who include Krishna among the visitors at the Nativity.

'a horse stood': these lines describe decorations on a spear. Cf. the (far more) elaborate description of Achilles' shield in book 18 of the *Iliad*.

'flew as a headless chicken': after the death of God, the world is returning to chaos. The following lines are borrowed from poems about Lemminkäinen, who also died and was revived; and from Sampo poems in which its owners are lulled to sleep.

'The Creator rose from death': this final episode places the Harrowing of Hell after the Resurrection, for Eastern Christianity lacks the Apostles' Creed (see note on A Glad Song About Jesus, p.245).

p.62 The Human Face. The epigraph echoes the hymn to light at the beginning of *Paradise Lost* book 3, where Milton regrets that he can no longer see 'flocks, or herds, or human face divine'.

p.65 The Hanged Maid. This poem, sung to Lönnrot by an old woman of Archangel Karelia, who scraped a living knitting stockings, is the basis of canto 4 of the *Kalevala*, one of the most affecting in the epic. Aino, sister of Joukahainen, is claimed as his prize by Väinämöinen for winning the singing match (canto 3). Her mother is delighted at the prospect of such a son-in-law, but Aino goes off and drowns herself, to reappear as a mermaid (canto 5). In Matro's poem the girl is plain Anni, pursued by the obscure Osmonen/Kalevainen, who frustrates her mother's wishes by hanging herself. This quite separate poem has an Estonian parallel in which a girl (whose name we do not know because she speaks for herself) stabs her pursuer dead and is congratulated by her family for getting rid of an upper-class pest.

'bath-whisks': bunches of birch twigs used to stimulate sweat in the sauna.

p.69 A Song in Finland. This and other poems by the same author have been adopted as folk songs.

p.71 A Glad Song About the Growth of the Finnish Tongue. One of the triumphs of Finnish peasant poetry; see foreword.

p.74 Lemminkäinen. This poem, collected from a village north of Lake Ladoga in 1845, was incorporated into the second, final edition (1849) of the *Kalevala*. There are three episodes:

1. The young tearaway Lemminkäinen sets out on a perilous journey to a feast to which he has not been invited (cf. canto 26, where the feast is transposed from Väinölä – Väinö/Väinämöinen's place – to Pohjola, the North Land, where it becomes Ilmarinen's wedding feast; Christian references are removed in keeping with the epic's supposed prehistoric chronology; and the incest is transferred to Kullervo). Before he leaves, Lemminkäinen boasts that his hairbrush bleeding will be a sign that he is in trouble (cf. canto 12, where he makes the boast before going off to woo a second wife).
2. Väinämöinen tells Lemminkäinen he is not welcome and promptly consigns him to death (cf. canto 27, where Lemminkäinen kills his host after a duel of magic and mayhem; and canto 14, where Lemminkäinen is killed by a herdsman he has insulted and is flung into the river of Tuonela; in the epic, Väinämöinen and Lemminkäinen are friends and allies).
3. The hairbrush bleeds, and Lemminkäinen's mother goes off in search of him. She finds him dead in the river, but he tells her to leave him there (cf. canto 15, where she resurrects him).

p.84 The Great Fire of Turku. The cathedral, begun in the 13th century, has survived many conflagrations. The 1827 fire destroyed what remained of its medieval interior, but it is now fully restored.

p.86 Elegy. Written while Lönnrot was collecting folk poetry in Archangel Karelia, 1837; see foreword.

p.87 *from the* Kalevala. The greatest event in the history of Finnish literature was the publication in 1835 of the first version of this monumental epic, assembled by Elias Lönnrot, a district health officer working in the northeast of the Grand Duchy. In 1935, to celebrate the centenary, the name of one of the 'singing villages', Uhtua, was changed to Kalevala; it was where Matro knitted her stockings. The epic is a reworking of oral poetry into a more or less continuous narrative. Lönnrot had taken his cue from a male bard who interrupted the heroic song he was singing to announce that the next part of the story consisted of wedding songs and 'you'll get them from the women'. Such a stitching together of songs had been done in ancient Greece by professional singers of Homeric epic known as rhapsodes (from *rhapto* 'I stitch'). Lönnrot – a tailor's son, fittingly enough – went on to publish the *Kanteletar* (q.v.) and in 1849 the final version of the *Kalevala*: incorporating material supplied by fellow collectors, the epic had grown to nearly 23,000 lines, twice its original size.

The canto given here (41) tells the mythical origin of the kantele, a kind of zither or psaltery widespread in the Baltic region. Thanks to the *Kalevala*, the kantele became the Finnish national instrument, despite the fact that folk musicians had long since abandoned it for the louder fiddle; today, however, the kantele is an option in music colleges, thanks largely to the effort of Martti Pokela and his family. The *Kalevala* tells how the boat in which our heroes set out to recapture the Sampo from the North Land (Pohjola; see note p.247) gets stuck on the back of a giant pike; this is duly killed and eaten, and its jawbone is fashioned into the first kantele.

p.94 *from the* Kanteletar. For the kantele, see above; the feminine suffix *-tar/tär* here refers to its resident spirit, a kind of muse. Lönnrot gave this name to his collection of oral lyrics and non-heroic narrative poems (broadly, ballads) which he published (1840-41) as a companion work to the *Kalevala*. The sexual polarity of epic/lyric poetry, often found in oral traditions, is not so sharply defined in the Finnish area: as men's songs declined, women took them over, and women's songs were used by men to express tender feelings.

Sibelius made a number of *Kanteletar* settings, of which the best known is *Rakastava* ('The Lover'), Op.14; and Yrjö Kilpinen made 64 solo settings, Op.100.

p.99 *Lullaby* represents a whole genre that still baffles scholars: why should a mother wish her baby dead? One view is that she wishes a better world for it, but the only language available to describe such a world is that of the otherworld; another view is that, in a society with a high infant mortality rate, she is taking out magical insurance, as actors wish their colleagues luck before a performance by saying 'Break a leg!'

p.99 *St Stephen* is an episode from 'The Ballad of the Virgin Mary', a long sequence of legends. This apocryphal account of the First Martyr has a parallel in the English carol 'King Herod and the Cock' (No.54 in *The Oxford Book of Carols*).

p.105 *On Rich and Poor* is from the ill-fated 1887 edition of the *Kanteletar*. As with the *Kalevala*, Lönnrot wanted to produce a second, larger edition, but he lived to complete only the ballad section. When this posthumous edition appeared, it was considered disproportionate, and anyway Lönnrot's approach to his material was judged out of date. The now standard edition (1901) adds ten ballads from 1887 as a supplement: the present poem is not included, but it deserves a place because of its rare theme of social justice. It is related to the aetiological myth about winter darkness in canto 49 of the *Kalevala*.

p.110 The Cricket. Like his contemporary John Clare, Kallio sees into the life of small creatures and learns from them. This poem retells – in oral metre – Aesop's (and La Fontaine's) fable of the cicada and the ant, but in favour of the former.

pp.112ff. *from* Idylls and Epigrams. 'She came back from her sweetheart's tryst': set by Sibelius, Op.37 No.5.

The girl's seasons: set by Sibelius as *Arioso*, Op.3.

The first kiss: set by Sibelius, Op.37 No.1.

The one moment: set by Oskar Merikanto, Op.36 No.1. This composer's songs are still much sung by Finns.

p.115 *from* Legends. *The Church* explores the essentially pagan idea that God can be (is best?) worshipped in solitude in the open air; cf. Dafydd ap Gwilym, *Offeren y Llwyn* ('The Woodland Mass').

'Onni': the Finnish name means 'luck'.

'Midsummer Day': the pagan festival, long since absorbed by Christianity as the feast of St John the Baptist, now a public holiday weekend known as *Juhannus*.

'The time of flowers is coming': the hymn, of Swedish origin, is No.557 in the standard Finnish hymn book.

p.119 *from* A Small Destiny. *Since then I have asked no more*: set by Sibelius, Op.17 No.1 – see foreword.

p.120 *from* Tales of Ensign Stål. *The Fifth Day of July* commemorates the battle of Hörnefors in northern Sweden in 1809, when a detachment of Finnish soldiers fell to the Russians.

p.124 Children's Song. Adopted as a folk song. The first line became the title of a famous trilogy of novels (1959-62) by Väinö Linna.

p.125 The Golden Bride. Miihkali Perttunen, known as Blind Miihkali, was the son of Arhippa (see p.246). The Golden Bride theme may have its origins in a cult object widespread in the Arctic: St Stephen of Perm mentioned a 'golden woman' among the idols of the 14th-century Komi. In the Finnish area it gets a variety of treatments. In Ingria the smith Ismaro, ridiculed (like Hephaestus) for his humble craft, makes magic objects to gain prestige; in Archangel Karelia (where Miihkali lived) the smith Ilmollini, rejected in love or widowed, tries and fails to make himself a wife. This is the interpretation adopted for the smith Ilmarinen in canto 37 of the *Kalevala*.

p.128 Christmas Song. Set by Sibelius, Op.1 No.4, and regularly sung during the festive season.

p.130 The Visit to Tuonela. Again from Archangel Karelia, this poem shows Väinämöini (Väinämöinen) in his role of shaman, mediating between worlds; the reference to churchgoing should be no surprise. Journeys to the otherworld (Tuonela = Tuoni's place = Manala = Mana's place) were undertaken by a shaman in a trance, to gain knowledge and hence power (here symbolised as tools) from a dead predecessor. The daughters of Tuoni are 'iron-clawed, iron-fingered' because ironworking was regarded with awe and suspicion by the shaman, who dealt in bones and stones;

like other female figures in Finnish myth, they combine numinous activities (spinning like the Fates) with such everyday tasks as washing clothes. As for knowledge, it is enough that the shaman has gained entry to the otherworld, and by his magic has returned to this world – though he has no further trouble with his sledge. The poem ends with a warning not to meddle with the dead (and deprive the shaman of his power). The questioning of Väinämöinen (from an earlier variant) surfaces in canto 16 of the *Kalevala*, where he goes to Tuonela for magic to finish building a boat – the subject of Sibelius' abandoned opera; the broken sledge episode occurs at the end of canto 25, without the church reference and the warning.

p.133 The Rapid-Shooter's Brides (see foreword) is a kind of home-grown Lorelei legend, set by Sibelius, Op.33 (unhelpfully known as *The Ferryman's Brides*). A nixie is a female nix, a Germanic water elf.

p.135 Finnish Sonnet introduced the form to Finland only in 1854, though it had been established in Sweden since the mid-17th century. Oksanen attributes its late appearance to the power of oral tradition, and to climate, invoking (though not by name) Petrarch. The form has remained a rarity in Finland.

p.136 Advice to a Bride: cf. *Kalevala* canto 23. The bard's name, Larin Paraske, means Lari's (her husband's) Paraske.

p.137 For a Sprain. This charm was current across northern Europe during the Dark Ages. Its earliest known form is the second of two pagan 'Merseburg charms' (9th century), among the first Old High German texts (*Phol ende Uuodan vuorun zi holza...*):

> Phol and Wodan were riding in the forest
> when Balder's foal sprained its foot.
> Then quoth Sinthgunt and Sun her sister,
> then quoth Frija and Volla her sister,
> then quoth Wodan as he knew how
> as well for bone-sprains, blood-sprains, limb-sprains:
> 'Bone to bone, blood to blood,
> limb to limbs, as if they were glued!'

p.139 Why I Have Come Here. In oral tradition, terms like rejoicing and merrymaking often mean no more than singing. Here the bard is saying that her job is not to express herself, but to entertain others.

p.140 The Far Forest introduces Kivi's neo-Classical prosody (see foreword), each unrhymed stanza matched foot for foot.

p.144 Song of My Heart. Each stanza consists of a rhymed couplet, followed by a line in one form of oral metre. The poem, sung in *Seven Brothers* by a mother with 'second sight', echoes the tradition of the *Kanteletar* lullaby 'Rock, rock my dark one' (p.99; note p.249).

p.145 The Rajamäki Regiment. The realism of Kivi's prose here happily enters his poetry. The increasingly idealised Finnish peasant gives way to a rowdy gipsy family; the kantele yields to the fiddle. Cupping is an ancient form of blood-letting. A shoat is a weaned piglet.

p.150 In Praise of Idleness is a splendid set of elegiacs expressing senti-
ments not readily associated with a Protestant society; even the sin of
omission gets short shrift. Suonio, alias Julius Krohn, fathered no less
than five writers, of whom Kaarle is better known (like his father) as a
folklorist, and Aino Kallas, who lived in London as the wife of the Estonian
ambassador, wrote (among much else) some spine-chilling short novels.
p.151 The Queen Delivered. A patriotic allegory set as a cantata by Sib-
elius, Op.48. To avoid the attention of the Russian censor, the piece was
billed at its first performance (1906) as 'Therein a Queen is Singing'.
p.154 Christmas Eve. Now a popular carol. Erkko is another poet whose
work has achieved folk song status.
p.154 Flowers at Pincio. One of Rome's Seven Hills, Pincio is a public
park.
p.155 Maiden, Sing. Set by Oskar Merikanto, Op.30 No.2 (first 3 stanzas
only).
p.156 Bird of Grief. Set by Oskar Merikanto, Op.36 No.2.
p.157 Ilkka celebrates the leader of the War of Clubs (Nuijasota), a peasants'
revolt in 1596 against Marshal Klaus Fleming, who after the 1570-95 war
between Sweden and Russia refused to demobilise his army.
p.159 At Christmas Time. Now a popular carol.
p.160 Spring in Karelia. Another adopted folk song. In its progress to its
present status (on the wave of Karelianism, a Romantic-nationalist pas-
toral movement with which Sibelius was associated) 'helpless' in the first
– and last – stanza was replaced by the more positive 'bottomless'.
p.161 Skating on the Sea: literally 'On Skates', but not everyone can skate
on the sea. Finnish taste is now responding to Manninen's command of
metaphor.
p.165 Diogenes. A rare sonnet about the Cynic philosopher who lived in
a barrel and snarled at worldly ambition.
p.167 Jean Sibelius. Written for the composer's 50th birthday (1915).
p.168 Jardin d'Acclimatation: the Paris zoo in the Bois de Boulogne. A
Nazirite was an ancient Hebrew partisan like Samson, who swore not to
cut his hair until he had achieved his ends (Judges 16); sometimes con-
fused by Christians with a Nazarene.
p.171 The Liquid from the Tree of Life. Benaiah son of Jehoiada pro-
claimed Solomon king, and Zadok the priest anointed him (1 Kings 1).
p.173 The Sea Hurls a Roller... Man may feel at one with nature, but the
feeling is not reciprocated. Cf. Hardy's 'Wagtail and Baby'.
p.174 Väinämöinen's Song. Written for the centenary (1902) of Lönnrot's
birth, when a statue of him and Väinämöinen, the main character of the
Kalevala, was unveiled in Helsinki; it is still there. Many of Leino's early
poems take their cue from the epic, though here Väinämöinen is no more
than Wordsworth's 'man speaking to men', but a man 'granted the kantele'.
p.176 from Whitsongs. The Finnish title (Helkavirsiä) combines pagan and
Christian elements. The two books so titled (1903, 1916) consist of nar-

rative poems in oral metre. The three poems translated here are from the first book, regarded by many as Leino's best. *Ylermi*: 'y' is pronounced *ü*.

p.182 The Dark One. Kalma is yet another name of Tuoni/Mana, the lord of the otherworld. It became the equivalent of Hebrew *she'ol*.

p.185 Nocturne. The twinflower (Finnish *vanamo*), whose two small pink flowers spring from a forked stem, grows only in the North, including the Scottish Highlands. Carl von Linné (Linnaeus), the 18th-century Swedish founder of modern botany, named it *Linnaea borealis* after himself because it was his favourite plant. Sibelius celebrates it in a piano piece, Op.76 No.11.

p.186 Elegy. An extraordinary statement from a poet in his 30th year, even a self-styled neo-Romantic.

p.187 Marjatta's Stars. Marjatta is the virgin whose son outwits Väinämöinen and brings the *Kalevala* with its pagan world to an end. In this poem (1912) we see more of the transcendental aspect of Romanticism. It existed already in the speculations of Goethe and Wordsworth, among others; but it acquired a new focus under the vague heading of Symbolism. Leino's older contemporary Yeats ('we were the last Romantics') flirted with Gnosticism, while further north – and east, in Russia – Symbolism involved a preoccupation with higher states of consciousness. In Protestant Finland, Marjatta's stars have little to do with the Maris Stella; rather, they symbolise a world of 'universal ideas', to which the lovers in the poem aspire, but fail to reach. An attack on Finnish parochialism? In another poem from the same year, Leino calls Finnish *kyltyyri* (properly *kulttuuri*, but with a French accent) a *karrikatyyri*.

p.189 A Lonely Ski Track. Sibelius wrote piano music (1925) to accompany the recitation of this poem. He thought enough of it to arrange it for harp and strings (1948).

p.191 *from* Spring Symphony. Lehtonen became better known as a novelist. This surprising monologue in free verse, contemporary with 'Prufrock', shows his interest in speech as – in Professor Boase's phrase – *poésie à l'état brut*; it is also surely one of the most toothsome celebrations of food in Western poetry.

'Korkeasaari zoo': Helsinki zoo, on one of the city's many islands.

'Uspensky church': the Orthodox cathedral of the Assumption in Helsinki.

'purple-fishers': the speaker seems to confuse the common sea mussel with the purple-fish, called 'purple-mussel' in Finnish. The Phoenicians sold the juice of this rare mollusc as a dye to the Greeks (*porphyra*) and to the Romans (*murex*), the original royal purple.

p.194 In the Tropics. The poet expresses the frustrations of her sex, class and period in the image of a tropical flower, perhaps the queen-of-the-night or moon cactus (*Selenicereus grandiflorus*), already cultivated in European hothouses. The poet was married to the composer Leevi Madetoja (the 'L.' probably means 'Leevi's', Onerva was her first name; cf. Larin Paraske above), but she was the mistress and biographer of Leino.

p.195 Sonnet About the Finnish Language. The model is not Petrarch but the German Baroque poets, who imported the sonnet on the wings of the French alexandrine. Koskenniemi was a Germanist whose own poetry, once highly esteemed, has not worn well.

p.196 Finlandia. Finland's 'Land of Hope and Glory', written (1940) to Sibelius' tune in Op.26 from the turn of the century.

p.197 *from* Sun-Green. This revolutionary work appeared in 1933, somewhat late for the Dada invoked by the author, who was nonetheless older than Tristan Tzara.

p.198 Day cools... Södergran speaks so directly that there is little need for commentary beyond the foreword (q.v.); but her *Complete Poems* are available in English, translated with an introduction by David McDuff (Newcastle upon Tyne: Bloodaxe Books, 1984).

p.201 Conceptio Artis. Originally the title of a painting by Akseli Gallen-Kallela, the versatile artist best remembered for his *Kalevala* illustrations. He showed the painting in an exhibition he shared with Munch in Berlin in 1895, after which he destroyed it. But something of it survives in his jacket design for a novel by Adolf Paul, and in a review by one Paul Scheerbart: 'In a green area lies a sphinx draped in white, and a naked man is approaching it in order to catch it. We see the man only from the back – but brilliantly painted...the artist wishes to subject his art to his will...' See also foreword.

p.202 Dolce far niente. From *Jääpeili* ('The Ice Mirror', 1925), Hellaakoski's most influential collection. This poem, for all its avant-garde approach, shows him clinging to the handrail of rhyme, which he never completely abandoned.

p.203 *from* The Jaguar. The opening section of a poem by an idealist of the Left who worked with Södergran.

p.203 Machine Song. A naive celebration of the new machine age, owing more to Mayakovsky than to Marinetti, whose Futurism had links with Fascism; our poet's machine even has a Russian accent.

p.205 Child in Starlight. A delicate ambiguity: is the child Jesus or not?

p.206 Genesis. Set to music (1956) and rescued from oblivion by Aarre Merikanto, more interesting son of Oskar. For Lyy (pron. *lüü*) see foreword.

p.213 Arthur Honegger. French composer of *Pacific 231*, a *mouvement symphonique* (1923) suggested by an American locomotive. *J'aime les locomotives*, said the composer, *comme d'autres aiment les femmes ou les chevaux*. American trains, it should be added, are still much faster than most Finnish trains.

p.214 A Way of Reckoning Time. An unusual subject for a poet whose native land is made of granite, which does not form caves. The limestone 'way of reckoning (*räkna*) time' is unfamiliar to Finns.

p.217 In Folk Song Style. Which folk song style is uncertain. 'Timothy' is timothy grass, cat's tail (*Phleum pratense*), a common European grass

introduced into North America by one Timothy Hanson; a shampoo is
now made from it. The poem has been set to music by Aulis Sallinen.

p.218 Bach. The opening line (*On virta*) means 'There is a stream', but
Bach means 'stream'. The poem (1956) was the basis of an article by
Manner on 'the poet's difficulties in expression', printed the following
year during the heyday of Finnish Modernism. 'Bruno' and 'Pascal' seem
to be the 16th-century Italian philosopher and the 17th-century French
mathematician and Catholic apologist. Manner's article was translated (by
Herbert Lomas) in *Books from Finland* 4/1994.

p.220 Michal was Saul's daughter and David's wife, who after David's
victory over the Philistines despised him as he danced before the Lord
and was punished with childlessness (2 Samuel 6).

p.223 *from* The Courtyard. A sequence of poems (1969) about the inhabi-
tants of a block of flats built round a courtyard, a common feature of cen-
tral Helsinki. The work was a breakthrough for Finland-Swedish realism.

'Högholm': Finnish Korkeasaari, the island where Helsinki zoo is.

'cowberry': alias lingonberry, red whortleberry (*Vaccinium vitis-idaea*),
the berry responsible for the virgin birth in canto 50 of the *Kalevala*, with
which Finland-Swedes are said to be unfamiliar.

p.226 *from* Chaconne: 2 sections from a 14-section poem. A chaconne is a
Baroque dance form, a continuous set of variations on a harmonic sequence;
the greatest example is J.S. Bach's Chaconne in D minor for unaccompanied
violin, the last movement of the Partita BWV 1004.

p.228 *from* The Winter Palace. This sequence of nine poems (1959), highly
praised by John Ashbery and Hans Magnus Enzensberger, may be regarded
as Haavikko's masterpiece, in the medieval sense of a work that marks the
end of apprenticeship. It is a key text of Finnish Modernism, which, like
Modernism elsewhere, celebrates a culture whose future is in doubt. The
title refers to the Winter Palace in St Petersburg, the crowning glory of
what was to be the new capital opening Russia to the riches – in all senses
– of the West. That a Finn should turn to Russia in this way was startling
enough; but Haavikko puzzled his first readers further by making only
passing references to the palace. Cf. Eliot's use of his locations in *Four
Quartets*.

The nine hectares of the Winter Palace – built by Western architects –
are contracted to nine poems that explore the Western concept of language
as an alternative reality, of the poem as a possible habitation; the primary
meaning of *stanza* is 'room'. Finnish poetry has hitherto (apart from oral
tradition) consisted largely of messages in bottles; here is a poem whose
content is its form. The poet, guided by a bird like the poet of 'Burnt
Norton', sets off on a 'mad journey' to a 'region that is nowhere, / away
from this poem'; for 'I want to be silent about everything language is about'
(*Fourth Poem*, translated here). He seeks a world before speech, but he has
nowhere else to go: language is his world – or is it? A woman asks him
to make the poem into a 'winter dwelling' for her: perhaps she wants to

know whether he can support her. Because he cannot write like the French Romantic poet Musset, he makes a pact with the Devil and goes into business, where he is more 'at home', for 'This Palace is too narrow to turn over in during sleep'. An antipoem, then, based on outdated notions of poetry? Or a warning that language, however palatial, is not to be trusted? The whole of 'The Winter Palace' has been translated by Anselm Hollo in *Paavo Haavikko: Selected Poems* (Manchester: Carcanet Press, 1991) and by Herbert Lomas in *Contemporary Finnish Poetry* (Newcastle upon Tyne: Bloodaxe Books, 1991).

p.230 *from* Ten Poems from 1966. Uncharacteristically direct, these are about the death of Haavikko's first wife, the poet and novelist Marja-Liisa Vartio.

p.231 *from* The One-and-Twenty. Haavikko's excursions into larger poetic forms – epic and verse drama – have a more national character and are less exportable; but this anthology provides the context for at least one of them. *The One-and-Twenty* (1974) caused a national sensation: here was a poet reinterpreting Finnish myth in the light of history, and standing the map on its head. The myth is that of the Sampo (p.47, note p.246): Haavikko reads it as an account of an 11th-century Viking raid on Byzantium to steal its mint, whose money was the most stable; the mistress of the North Land becomes the Byzantine empress Zoe. While there is no evidence that Finns took part in the raid, scholars agree that the Sampo myth took shape around the time mentioned.

Section 10 of the 35-section poem deals with the theft itself by Vikings with colourful invented names. *Samppi, sammi*, 'bright-lid' reflect the confused references to the Sampo in oral tradition.

p.234 R.S. Thomas. One abrupt prophet's tribute to another. Like the author of *H'm*, Ågren identifies strongly with his depressed native region, Swedish-speaking Ostrobothnia in north-west Finland. He set up a cooperative to publish local writers, gaining national attention only in 1988, when he won the principal Finnish literary award, the Finlandia Prize.

p.238 *from* Poems from the Seabed. Reflecting Andersson's work as a psychotherapist. He is also a jazz pianist and Minister of Culture in the present government.

p.240 *from* The Dance Floor on the Mountain. 'Aridela! Arihagne!' Coming from a translator of *Ulysses*, these may be Joycean puns on the (arid) island of Naxos where Theseus abandoned Ariadne after she had helped him kill the Minotaur. Cf. 'Suffoclose! Shikespower! Seudodanto! Anonymoses!' in the Ballad of Persse O'Reilly, early on in *Finnegans Wake*.